TEN GIRLS
WHO MADE
HISTORY

LIGHT KEEPERS

Irene Howat

© copyright 2003 Christian Focus Publications
ISBN: 1-85792-837-7
reprinted 2004
Published by Christian Focus Publications
Geanies House, Fearn, Ross-shire
IV20 1TW, Great Britain
www.christianfocus.com
e-mail:info@christianfocus.com
Cover Design by Alister Macinnes
Cover Illustration by Elena Temporin,
Milan Illustrations Agency
Printed and bound in Great Britain
by Cox & Wyman, Reading

All incidents retold in these stories are based on true situations. Where specific information about childhood incidents has been unobtainable the author has written these paragraphs using other information concerning family life, hobbies, home life and relationships freely available in other biographies.

All rights reserved. No part of this publication may be reproduced, stored in a retrieval system, or transmitted, in any form, by any means, electronic, mechanical, photocopying, recording or otherwise without the prior permission of the publisher or a license permitting restricted copying. In the U.K. such licenses are issued by the Copyright Licensing Agency, 90 Tottenham Court Road, London W1P 9HE.

Cover illustration: This depicts Henrietta Mears as a young girl. When she suffered from muscular rheumatism she often had to sit inside and watch her friends enjoying fresh air and exercise outside. But after she was healed she said to her sister, 'I learned a lot in those two years. I've especially learned to trust my future to God and not to fret about it. But that doesn't stop me wondering what he has in store for me.'

for
Muriel and Matthew

Contents

Contents

Mary Jane Kinnaird

The little girl looked round the circle of her brothers and sisters. Their faces all reflected the flickering of the coal fire, and their eyes seemed to dance with the light from it. There were six in the family, and she was the youngest of them all by several years. It was Christmas time, and they had gathered at their grandparents where they could spend some time together. Sir Gerard Noel and Lady Barham loved their grandchildren dearly.

'It's very sad,' Mary Jane said. 'You can all remember Papa and Mama and I can't remember them at all.'

Her oldest sister turned in her direction.

'I was very upset when they died,' she said. 'And I remember feeling especially sad for you because I knew you wouldn't have any memories of them.'

'Tell me about them,' the child pleaded. 'Then I can imagine that I knew them.'

Mary Jane's oldest sister took charge.

'Let's go round the circle and each tell

something that we remember about our parents. You start,' she said, to her brother.

'Papa was a banker,' the lad said.

'And he always wore very smart clothes,' said the next along.

'Mama was gentle and kind,' Mary Jane's sister added.

'And she was quite a serious person,' commented her brother.

'Mama was very kind,' the oldest sister said. 'In fact, Mary Jane, although you don't remember her, you are really very like Mama. You are gentle and kind and serious. So despite not knowing her at all, there is something of Mama in you.'

That night Mary Jane went to bed happier than she had felt for some time because over the weeks that had gone before, she had thought a lot about not knowing her parents.

'The holiday's over now, I'm afraid,' said Miss Holloway. 'And I think we should start today with your piano lesson.'

Mary Jane smiled at her governess. She had played the piano for her brothers and sisters many times over the holiday and had learned a new tune. Sitting down at the piano, she began to play. Miss Holloway's eyes opened wide, then a smile played on her face.

'Who taught you that tune?' she asked, delightedly.

'My brother William,' the child said. 'He

said it would be a nice surprise for you.'

'He was quite right,' laughed Miss Holloway. 'And I would really enjoy hearing it over again.'

Happy that she had pleased her governess, Mary Jane settled back at the piano and began to play. Mary Jane's brother, who had taught her the tune, came into the room as his little sister played.

'Well done, Twinkle,' he said, clapping at her performance.

The little girl's face broke into a wide smile. Her older brothers and sisters may have had homes and families of their own but there was something special about their times together at Grandma and Grandpa's. It was Mary Jane's home and she loved it, but she loved it even more when all the family was there... and she adored William, even if he did call her that awful pet name!

'I suggest you write your thank-you letters this afternoon,' Miss Holloway said, as they finished the morning's school work. 'You have one to write to your godmother and one to your uncle.'

Although Mary was a clever child, she neither read nor wrote quickly. So the writing of two thank-you letters took some time. After she had finished telling her godmother how much she liked the gift she had sent her, there was still a lot of empty paper on the page. As she thought what else she could say, an idea came to her mind and she wrote it down before it escaped.

'I hope that whenever you call, I shall be able to say my catechism (Bible questions and answers) perfectly.'

Then, signing her name, she folded the paper, glad that the job was done.

'She really does like learning her catechism,' Miss Holloway thought, as she checked the letter for spelling mistakes. 'Young though Mary Jane is, I think she is a Christian.'

By the time Mary Jane was 15 years old, she had begun to keep a diary. And her diary shows that she thought a lot about what it meant to be a Christian.

'December 3, 1831 – This week I've not prayed nearly enough for other people! One night I was very unkind and I've let little things annoy me. Every day when we've had family prayers, my mind has wandered all over the place. And I've wasted a lot of time too.'

'December 10, 1831 – I think that pride is my biggest sin and it shows itself in so many ways. Sometimes I feel so unthankful and discontented. And often I forget about God.'

'December 17, 1831 – The Bible says we should copy Jesus, and I hardly do that at all. He was so kind, and I'm only kind to people I really like.'

But if anyone else had read Mary Jane's

Mary Jane Kinnaird

diary they might have thought she was being very hard on herself, for the teenager was kind and gentle, and really did seem to try to live the kind of life a young Christian person should live.

'I think it is time we bought you some new dresses,' Lady Barham told her youngest granddaughter.

Mary Jane looked at herself in the mirror.

'This dress is fine,' she said. 'And my other dresses will do another year too. I've not grown quickly this last while.'

Lady Barham sat down and looked at the girl.

'I still think you need new dresses. These ones may still fit you, but they don't fit the fashion. You don't want to look old-fashioned at your age surely!'

Although she didn't care at all about fashion, Mary Jane agreed to go to her grandmother's dressmaker. But she found it difficult to endure an afternoon of looking at cloth that didn't interest her, deciding on styles she couldn't care less about, and being pinned and tucked into boredom. It was with the greatest relief that the fitting was done, and she could put on her old blue dress and go home. By the time her new dresses were delivered she had forgotten all about them.

'I don't know what we'll do with Mary Jane,' Lady Barham commented to her husband, 'she just doesn't care about the things most girls her age are interested in. I often wonder what she will do with her life.'

When Mary Jane was 21 years old, she went to live with her uncle, Rev Baptist Noel. She just loved sitting at the table and listening to him talk. Fancy dresses didn't matter in his home, there were much more interesting things for a girl to be thinking about.

'I visited a rookery in St Giles today,' Uncle Noel told her one day.

'Tell me about it,' Mary Jane said. 'I want to know how poor people really live.'

Uncle Noel looked at his niece and knew she was telling the truth. He sat down beside her on the window seat and told her what he had seen.

'I suppose rookeries get their name because they are very tall and narrow buildings, although it's hard to imagine anything less like a tree covered with rooks' nests. The one I visited today had over 300 people living in it, and every one of them desperately poor. Sometimes several families live in one room. I heard of one small room where five families lived, one family in each corner and another in the middle of the room. When someone asked how they managed, the husband of one of the corner families said that it had been fine until the family in the middle of the room took in a lodger. The poverty is terrible,' he concluded, 'but what is worse is that hardly any person in the rookery I visited knows that Jesus can save their souls.'

'Is that why you helped to start the London City Mission two years ago?' Mary Jane asked.

Uncle Noel looked at the serious girl at his side. 'Yes,' he said. 'That's why I hope that the London City Mission will be a great success. They will employ ordinary people rather than ministers to go out to the ordinary people of London.'

'I'll pray for the missionaries,' promised Mary Jane.

And Uncle Noel knew that she would.

In 1841, just four years after she had moved to her uncle's home, Mary Jane founded an organization of her own. It was the St John's Training School for Domestic Servants. As each girl came for training, Mary Jane took down her details and kept a record of the work she did. And she continued to do that for many years, until over 1000 young women had passed through her training school.

Not only that, she used a lot of her own money to fund the training as well as raising funds from her friends. Even when she married the Honourable Arthur Kinnaird, when she was 26 years old, her interest in helping people continued.

Over the years that followed, Mary Jane tried to interest her friends in the things that interested her and not fashions that she could never be bothered with. She sent out invitations for tea and discussion, and the discussions were on serious topics.

Her invitation for one Wednesday in May 1848, listed that afternoon's topics as:

1. Christian education – especially for ragged and poor children.

2. The problems of British colonies.

3. How to improve conditions for the people of London.

4. How to spread the good news of Jesus in Europe.

The following Wednesday her friends were invited to discuss:

1. Education.

2. Emigration.

3. Young men in towns.

4. Problems of people living in the countryside.

Having tea with Mary Jane Kinnaird could be hard work!

Because she could not remember her mother, when Mary Jane's children were born she worked hard at being a good mother.

Mary Jane Kinnaird

'I know the fashion is only to see your children for a short time before they go to bed,' she told her husband, 'but I won't have that in our home. They can come into my room anytime without knocking.'

Sir Arthur looked rather shocked.

'You'll never have any peace,' he said. 'They'll run in and out all day.'

Mary Jane smiled. 'I hope they do.'

Lady Kinnaird was the kind of mother she would have wished to have herself. Whatever she was doing, her children were welcome. Every night she prayed with them as they went to bed, whatever was going on in the house and no matter what important people were staying. Even as her children grew older they were constantly in her thoughts and prayers. Amazingly, when her son went off to boarding school, she wrote a letter to him every single day!

During the Crimean War, in 1854-55, Lady Kinnaird became aware of a problem. And with two friends she set out to do something about it.

'I hear that soldiers injured in the Crimea are not receiving the care they need, and many are dying unnecessarily,' she told her friends.

'I know,' one agreed. 'What they need are trained nurses to go out there and help.'

'But where would we find trained nurses?' asked the other.

'We wouldn't find them anywhere,' said Lady Kinnaird. 'We'd train them here in London them send them out when they knew what they were doing.'

A building was found and a home opened where young women in training would live. That was when Florence Nightingale became involved, and the two women worked together from then on.

'It's all very well training nurses for the Crimea,' Mary Jane said to her husband. 'But what will happen when the war is over?'

'I suppose they'll go back home to their families,' he suggested, though he was quite sure that was not what his wife had in mind.

'Young women will still need to come to London to train as nurses or to work,' Lady Kinnaird thought aloud, 'and we could provide a home where they could live simply and safely, like the nurses' home.'

'Talk it over with your friends,' said Sir Arthur. 'See what they think.'

Lady Kinnaird wrote to several friends the following day – as she still read and wrote slowly it took most of the afternoon – and invited them for tea and discussion. The topic was to be 'providing a home for young women who come to London for training or employment.'

A small organisation was founded which soon joined with another and became the

Mary Jane Kinnaird

Young Women's Christian Association. Lady Kinnaird was president. The YWCA (as it was soon called) was not an instant success. Those who believed in it had to work hard to make it work. But it did work, and over the years homes were opened in other cities as well as London. Mary Jane Kinnaird didn't live to see it, but eventually the YWCA spread to many different countries, and provided homes for hundreds of thousands of young women who had to move to cities to study or work.

'I've just heard the most awful news,' Lady Kinnaird told her daughter. 'There have been some terrible murders in Whitechapel in London. I know I'm dying and can't do anything to help keep the girls of Whitechapel safe, but you could open a home for them.'

Mary Jane was right, she was dying. Even in the last few days of her life she encouraged her daughter to take over from where she left off. So when Lady Mary Jane Kinnaird died and went home to Jesus, her work on earth went on. A place of safety was opened in Whitechapel. It was called the Kinnaird Rooms.

Fact File: *The Crimean War*. This war was fought on the Crimean peninsula, which is in the Black Sea between Turkey and Russia. The war is well known for the unnecessary loss of life caused by lack of organisation. The troops were sent out without adequate food, equipment or medical supplies. When the nurses arrived in the Crimea, they found that the hospital had no medicine, bandages or cleaning materials. The work of the nurses who went out made a huge difference to how injured soldiers were cared for.

Keynote: Mary Jane was well off and could have spent her time thinking about things like dresses and parties. However, she was very concerned for the welfare of the poor. She didn't stop helping when the crisis of the Crimean War was over: she was willing to carry on the work afterwards. It is important that we should try to help people and to do it all the time, even when it is hard and there is no one to praise us for doing it.

Think: Although Mary Jane was very busy trying to help all sorts of people, she did not forget her own family. She was always willing to see her children, no matter what she was doing, and she wrote to her son at boarding school every day. Do you think that he always wrote back? She would have been very pleased if he had. Think about ways in which you can show kindness and affection to those who try to help you, and make sure that you don't take them for granted.

Prayer: Lord Jesus, thankyou for being willing to make sacrifices and to suffer so that you can save people from their sins. Thankyou for helping those whom important people usually ignored. Please teach me not to be selfish and help me to do all that I can to help others. Amen.

Emma Dryer

Emma stood at the window while her mother brushed her long hair.

'One, two three, four ...' she counted, as the brush tugged.

'Five, six, seven, seventy seven, seventy eight...' the girl continued.

'I don't think so,' Mrs Dryer said. 'Your hair needs brushed a hundred times every day to make it shine. And you don't get to a hundred by missing out all the numbers between seven and seventy seven!'

Emma grinned. Sometimes her mother's mind was so far away when she brushed her hair that the girl got off with her trick of missing out numbers.

'I'll not skip so many tomorrow,' decided Emma. 'If I miss out just a few here and there she'll not notice.'

'Are you ready for church?' Mr Dryer called, from the bottom of the stair.

Pulling her hat down on her newly brushed

hair, Emma dashed out of her room and down to her father.

'Ready!' she said, snapping her feet to attention in front of him.

'And so you are ... not,' her father smiled. 'Your hair is brushed, your hat and coat are on, but they look really funny with your pink slippers!'

Emma glanced down, and where her polished brown boots should have been there was a pair of pink knitted slippers.

'Quick as you can!' her father said, pushing her gently in the direction of the stairs.

'One, two, three, four ...' Emma counted, as she ran up, and 'eleven, twelve, thirteen,' as she landed at the bottom again.

'Let's go,' said Mr Dryer, taking his daughter by the hand.

Mrs Dryer, who was not feeling very well, stayed at home that day.

'Let's play the number game,' Emma suggested, as they set out on their walk to church. 'You be it.'

This was the girl's favourite game because she had invented it herself. The person who was 'it' had to give a number and the other person had to guess which story the number came from and then tell the story.'

Emma Dryer

Mr Dryer thought for a minute. 'What story does 99 come from?' he asked.

'That's easy,' laughed Emma. 'It's the story Jesus told about the shepherd who had 100 sheep. One went missing, and that left only 99. The shepherd searched for the missing sheep until he found it. Then he carried it all the way home.'

'Your turn now,' her father said.

Emma screwed up her face as she tried to think of a hard one. Then she grinned. 'What story does twelve come from?' she asked.

'Is it about the disciples?' queried her father.

The girl shook her head.

'Is it about Jacob's sons?'

'That's right,' laughed Emma. 'Now you've got to tell me the story.'

By the time Mr Dryer had finished the long story of Jacob and his twelve sons, the pair of them were nearly at church.

'Will you tell me about the service?' Mrs Dryer asked her husband, when they arrived back home.

Emma had gone upstairs to take off her coat, hat and boots.

Mr Dryer told his wife about the hymns, the Bible readings, and the sermon.

'And what was Emma chatting about as you walked?' she asked.

'We played her number game on the way there, and on the way back we talked about the people who were at the service.'

'I've never known a child so fascinated by numbers,' Mrs Dryer said. 'She counts everything, even the peas in their pods when she's shelling them! And it's all your fault,' she concluded, smiling.

'My fault?' puzzled her husband.

'Yes, indeed. Don't you remember the first thing you taught her when she was just a few months old?'

He shook his head.

'You cuddled her on your knee, and taking every one of her tiny toes in turn, you counted up to ten and down again, tickling her each time you finished! Before she was a year old, she was counting them with you.'

Mr Dryer laughed. 'I had no idea I was launching her on a career in mathematics!'

But Emma's happy home life was not to last for many years. While she was still a girl, both of her parents died and Emma was sent to live with her aunt in New York State. Although her aunt was kind to her, sometimes the girl felt very sad. Often she went for long walks on her own, and as she walked she remembered walks with her parents and the word and number games they had played together. Sometimes the memories made her

Emma Dryer

feel warm inside, and other times they made her want to cry.

'Be sure you're home before dark,' Emma was often told, as she left on her walks.

'Aunt,' the girl said early one evening. 'I always come home before dark because you tell me to, but I'd really like to stay out later this evening.'

'Why's that?' she was asked.

Realising that her aunt was worried, the teenager smiled broadly.

'I won't get up to mischief,' she giggled. 'It's just that I love being out in the starlight. Often I sit for hours with my room window open just watching the stars, and tonight I'd like to walk for a while in the starlight.'

He aunt laughed. 'I don't think you'll come to any harm doing that,' she agreed.

As Emma grew older, two things fascinated her: mathematics and the stars. She made up number puzzles for her classmates, and some of them were so hard their teacher had to work them out. And, in the late evenings, when the stars shone, Emma drew plans of the constellations, and sky maps of the different times of year.

'What do you want to do with your life?' her aunt asked, when Emma was nearly grown up. 'I expect you want a handsome and rich husband and a houseful of happy children.'

The girl smiled.

'I suppose I might want that one day,' she agreed. 'But right now I'd like to go to college to study mathematics and astronomy.'

Emma's aunt nodded. 'I thought that's what you would say. And there's no reason why in this modern age you should not do just that. When I was a girl in the 1810s things were different. Not many girls went on to study after they left school in those far off days.'

From school Emma went to a women's college, and from there she went to university. She was such a brilliant student that she became a university teacher and eventually she was appointed Head of the Woman's Faculty of Illinois State Normal University.

'I wish my parents had lived to know how well I've done,' she found herself thinking, when she heard the news that she had got the job. 'They would have been so pleased to see me settled for life in such a secure position.'

In 1870, when Emma was 35 years old, something happened that changed things. In fact, she almost lost her life to typhoid fever. Emma was already a Christian by then, but the seriousness of her illness made her do some very hard thinking.

Emma Dryer

'How are you feeling today?' Martha asked, when she came to visit.

Still too weak to raise her head from the pillow, Emma smiled in her friend's direction.

'I'm feeling a bit better,' she said. 'And I think I'm going to live after all.'

'Of course you're going to live,' scolded Martha.

Emma's face grew serious. 'There's no of course about it,' she stated simply. 'I know I nearly died. And of this I'm sure, someone who has come so close to death can't just pick up the pieces and go on as they were going before.'

Martha looked concerned. 'Is she still a little delirious?' she wondered.

Some months later Martha and Emma were deep in conversation.

'You're looking wonderfully well despite your brush with death,' Martha announced. 'In fact, you're absolutely back to normal.'

'I thank God for healing me,' smiled Emma. 'And for showing me the direction in which I should go.'

'Direction?' queried her friend. 'What do you mean?'

Emma took a deep breath before breaking her news.

'I believe that God is leading me to give up my job and work full time for him.'

'Give up your job!' gasped her astonished friend. 'But you've got a wonderful, well-paid, important position. You can't just give it all up like that!'

'I can,' Emma assured her. 'And I have. My notice has already been given.'

'Are you sure you're feeling all right?' Martha asked sincerely. She wondered if her friend's illness had returned and caused her to be confused.

'I'm feeling very well indeed,' Emma announced. 'In fact, I've never felt better or more content in all of my life.'

Later that year, Emma Dryer moved to Chicago and took up an unpaid job there.

'Dear Martha,' she wrote at the head of a sheet of paper. 'You've been so good to me you deserve a letter now that I've settled down in my new position. Let me tell you what life is like here. I'm lodging with a family, which is a new experience for me, and I'm enjoying it. However, I must admit that after the academic life I've led over the last few years, the hustle and bustle of a family home took a little getting used to! My job is befriending young women who are in trouble, and there is no end of them here in Chicago. Many are poor girls who've never had a chance in life. Others have got themselves into trouble of their own making. But

Emma Dryer

whatever the reason, they are in need of help and support. Of course, what they most need is a Saviour, and as often as I can I tell them about the Lord Jesus. Recently one young woman was very cross with me. She said that it was all right for me, coming from a happy and wealthy home, and that I couldn't possibly understand what life was like for 'ordinary' girls. When I explained to her that my parents died when I was very young and that I was brought up by an aunt, she settled down and we were able to have a really good talk. One last bit of news before I finish, I'm attending Illinois Street Church, which was founded by Dwight L. Moody, and I love it.'

'Dwight L. Moody,' thought Martha, when she read the letter. 'He's the most famous preacher in America. I wonder if Emma will ever meet him.'

Emma did meet Mr and Mrs Moody, and they became very good friends.

In 1871, a terrible fire blazed its way through the heart of Chicago, leaving whole streets just heaps of ash and charred timber.

'We've got to do everything we can to help,' Dwight Moody told a group who met to pray for the city. 'Let's raise as much money as we can to provide food, clothing and shelter for those who have been burned out of their homes.'

The prayer meeting turned into a planning meeting as people got their heads together to work out how best to help.

'I've a job specially for you,' Dwight told Emma. 'The Bible study class here is huge and your experience is needed to make it a really worthwhile training ground.'

'That won't help with fire damage,' she pointed out.

Moody agreed, then added that it would do more lasting good than building new houses.

Because she knew that Martha would have heard about the great fire, Emma wrote to assure her friend that she had not been injured.

'Although I was unaffected by the fire, it has changed the work I do,' she wrote. 'I'm now very involved in Bible teaching (though our church was burned down) and I also hold mothers' meetings and sewing classes for girls. Now, Martha, don't you be smiling at that! How my old university students would laugh if they could see me now! But I am where I believe God wants me to be, and I'm happy.'

Moody recognised in Emma a very clever women and a splendid teacher. He persuaded her to open a school where young women who felt called to home or foreign mission would be trained.

Emma Dryer

'Tell me about the training you do?' a visitor asked Emma.

'It is a one year course,' she explained. 'The students do a mixture of lectures and practical work here in Chicago. They do house-to-house visits, take meetings in homes and churches, help with Sunday Schools and mothers' meetings as well as doing what they can for the homeless poor people of the city.'

By 1878, 17 of Emma's former students were doing Bible Work in the city, and many others were missionaries abroad. Moody's dream was becoming reality. But his dream was bigger than Emma knew. He dreamed of a college for men and women, somewhere young people could be trained for two or three years, a college that would send missionaries to the furthest parts of the world to tell people about the Lord Jesus. It took a long time, and it was not always easy going, but the Bible school that Emma Dryer founded became the place that Dwight L. Moody dreamed of. Today The Moody Bible Institute in Chicago is one of the most famous missionary training colleges in the whole world.

Factfile: *Women in education.* Emma Dryer was a pioneer in education. For a long time people thought that university education was only for men. America, however, admitted women to university before the United Kingdom did. Emma was able to attend Illinois State Normal University but Oxford University did not admit women until 1878 (when Emma was 43) while men and boys had been going to Oxford University since the 12th century! Women like Emma have helped to overcome prejudice and now as many women go to university as men.

Keynote: Emma was very successful, and most people would have agreed with her friend Martha that she should settle down in her important job. She felt that God wanted her to do special work for him instead. It might have been very scary to give up everything that she had worked towards and move to the busy city of Chicago, but Emma did it and God helped her. Doing what God wants can be daunting. However, he will give us the strength to do what we should.

 Think: Although Emma had moved away from the university, her special skills came in useful later on when she helped to train young women who were called to work as missionaries abroad and in America. She could not see how God would tie everything together when she decided to go to Chicago, but God could. We don't always know what God will want us to do but he often wants us to use the skills that we have to serve him and to help others. Think about some of the skills that you have. How might God use these for his glory?

 Prayer: Lord Jesus, thankyou for the chance to learn about mathematics and science. Thankyou for giving me the opportunity to learn about you. Please help me to use all of the experiences that I have to serve you. Give me the courage to do what you tell me, even when it is hard or scary to do so. Amen.

Florence Nightingale

Florence and her sister were not sorry to be parted. They were so very different. Parthe (whose full name was Parthenope) loved parties and frilly dresses. Flo, as Florence was known, liked books and studying. Both thought the other was boring.

'I love staying with you,' Flo told her cousin Hilary. 'We do such exciting things!'

Hilary smiled cheekily.

'Would you like to come visiting today?'

Thinking that meant dressing up and sitting in parlours, Flo screwed up her face.

'No thanks,' she said. 'I get that at home.'

Her cousin giggled. 'Not that kind of visiting,' Hilary explained. 'My governess is visiting the poor today and I sometimes go with her. Do you want to come too?'

Flo, who was eight years old, knew about visiting the poor. Sometimes she went with her mother delivering food to the hungry.

'Yes, I'll come,' she said. 'I think I'd like that.'

'What a wonderful afternoon I've had,' Flo wrote in her diary before going to bed.

'Miss Johnson took us to a number of cottages where very poor people live. She actually goes INSIDE the cottages. They were so dark! Miss Johnson was very nice to the people, treating them like friends. And when we went into one cottage where there was a sick baby, she picked up the child and hugged him. Then she examined the poor little thing and said she'd bring medicine to help his chesty cough. I stroked the baby and he stopped crying. It felt wonderful to be really helping someone.'

Closing her diary carefully, Flo lay back on her pillows and thought over the day. She imagined herself as a grown-up, going from cottage to cottage with a basket of fruit and helping the sick people she visited. Before she knew it, had fallen asleep and begun dreaming, then it was morning and time to get up!

A few months later, in early 1829, dreadful news came to the Nightingale home. One of their little cousins had died. Both girls had been very fond of him. After the period of mourning was over, Parthe and Flo's governess, Miss Christie, decided that they needed something new to focus their energies on, something practical, fulfilling and creative.

Florence Nightingale

'I have a new project for you,' their governess said. 'I want you to do something to help the poor village people.'

'Cook will give us food to take to them,' announced Parthe. 'And the gardener can dig up some vegetables.'

'No,' Miss Christie said, 'I want you to think of ways of earning money so that you can do something for them yourselves.'

'Earning money?' quizzed Parthe, who knew she would never have to earn money in all her life. Her family was quite rich enough to keep her comfortably.

'I think that's a good idea,' Flo said. 'I'll embroider handkerchiefs and I could tidy Mum's threads for her. You could do some drawings to sell to our relatives,' she told her sister. 'You're brilliant at drawing.'

Over the weeks that followed, Parthe and Flo did all sorts of things and raised enough money to give the village children a party, complete with food and gifts to take home.

'I LOVE helping people,' Flo wrote in her diary. 'And I love keeping notes of everything I do and see. Perhaps one day I'll write a book.'

In 1831, when Flo was eleven years old, Miss Christie spoke to her very quietly. By the time Miss Christie had finished speaking tears were rolling down Flo's cheeks.

'You're leaving?' she said softly. 'You're leaving us to get married?'

'Yes,' the young woman said. 'But we will write, and we will pray for each other.'

Flo believed both these things would happen, but she knew that when Miss Christie left her life would change. Nothing would ever be the same again. If a tear smudged the ink in her diary that night, it was only one of the many that fell. But many more tears were shed the following year when her governess died in childbirth.

Praying was as much part of Flo's life as writing her diary, but in the weeks that followed her dear friend's death many of Flo's prayers were in the form of questions.

'Why did she die, Lord? Why could she and the baby not both have lived?'

Flo's grandmother came to stay some weeks later, and helping to look after the old lady helped the girl to get over her grief. In fact, helping people always helped Flo too. It gave her a good feeling.

'What will I do with my life?' Flo often asked herself. 'I can't just spend my time going to dinner parties and balls. And I'm not going to prance about in fancy gowns every day, that's for sure!' Night after night she prayed that God would make her useful. Then, on 7th February 1837, the Lord answered her prayers. The seventeen-year-old knew without a shadow of doubt that he had called her into his service. She didn't know what God would ask her to do, but she knew that something useful would come out of her life.

'You'll enjoy seeing where you were born,' Flo's father told her. 'In our grand trip round Europe we'll visit Florence, the city that gave you your name.'

Flo didn't particularly want to spend ages touring Europe, but that's what the family did. They took so much with them that her father's coach needed six horses to pull it! The Nightingales, servants and all, left home in September that year and didn't return for nineteen months! The most important event in the family diary after that was the day that Parthenope and Florence met the new young Queen Victoria.

Although Florence continued to live in high society, her interests lay elsewhere. 'Oliver Twist' had just been published, and this opened her eyes to the poverty in London. Her aunt was very involved in campaigning against slavery. Florence even started reading government reports on health, the employment of children and housing the poor! In fact, she was developing what is called a social conscience. That means that she was becoming aware of problems that really existed, and felt she wanted to help.

When she was 24, an American doctor and his wife visited the Nightingale home. He worked with deaf and blind people, but he also talked about work he wanted to do with those who were sick in body or mind. Florence could hardly wait to talk to him.

'Do you think a young English woman like me could work in a hospital?' she asked, at the first opportunity.

The doctor looked at Florence.

'It would certainly be most unusual for someone from your kind of family to do work like that,' he said. 'But if you think that's what you should be doing, go for it. And God will go with you.'

The young woman's heart pounded with excitement. From then on her mind was made up. God had called her into his service, and she would find a way of serving him.

It was not until 1853 that Florence found what she was wanting. That was when she became manager of the Institute for the Care of Sick Gentlewomen, and she only got the job because she had spent much of the previous few years nursing one or other aged or ill relative as well as spending a short time in a hospital in Germany.

'This is what I was made to do,' Flo told her cousin. 'This is my service to God.'

'What does the job involve?' her cousin asked.

Florence thought back over her first few months with the Institute.

'It has involved travelling to Paris to research nursing there. And here in London I've assisted in operations and cared for patients after their surgery. I've nursed women with tuberculosis, and I've tried my best to comfort those suffering from stress.'

'Is that all?' her cousin laughed jokingly.

Florence thought she was being serious. 'No,' she said, 'that's not quite all. I've also ordered the furniture for the Institute, put up shelves to hold things, kept the accounts and looked after the stores.'

Having looked for something useful to do, Florence Nightingale was now incredibly busy ... and loving it.

In March 1854, Britain and France declared war on Russia. The Crimean War had begun. Six months later a worrying report was published.

'Insufficient plans have been made for the care of the wounded. Not only are there not enough surgeons ... not only are there no dressers and nurses ... there are not even linens to make bandages.'

Just five days later, Florence Nightingale wrote to her cousin, 'A small private expedition of nurses has been organised for Scutari and I have been asked to command it. I believe we may be of use.'

Florence and her 37 nurses arrived just after a battle, and they could hardly believe what met them. As usual, she took very detailed notes.

'I've been given five damp rooms for my nurses. The dead body of a Russian general is in one of them, and rats are in all five. The men are fed with half-cooked meat soup and no vegetables at all. There are so many of them that the bath rota means each is bathed once every eighty days! Not only that, the same sponge is used to wash everyone.'

Utterly shocked, Florence set out to organise her nurses into some kind of useful order. Although the doctors were not too keen to have nurses helping them, Florence made sure they got down to work.

'Go to the market and buy as many vegetables as you can carry,' she told some of them.

'Set up the portable stoves we brought with us,' she instructed others, 'and get ready to cook some decent food for these poor men.'

'Wash these bandages, and rip more linen into strips,' she said to some who were still looking for jobs. 'Then wash anything in sight. Everything here is disgusting!'

The new nurses were hardly settled in, when news came of terrible losses at the Battle of Balaclava. Soon the number of injured doubled from 2,000 to 4,000 men.

Florence wrote to a friend in London, describing the scene.

'We now have four miles of beds, and not eighteen inches apart. ... As I did my night rounds among the wounded there was not one murmur, not one groan. These poor fellows bear pain with superhuman heroism.' Then, on the subject of cleanliness, she added, 'We have no basins, not a bit of soap, not a broom. I have ordered 300 scrubbing brushes!'

Florence Nightingale was far from timid. When she saw something needed done, she went all out to make sure it was done.

'Every patient should have his own bed,' she demanded, 'and they should all have exactly the right food for their condition.'

When objections were raised about how to do that, she had her answer ready.

'Ward masters will have to be appointed.

They will see to the running of their own wards, and make sure they are kept clean.'

'But... but...' the official tried to argue. However, he didn't stand a chance. Florence continued, 'The hospital needs a governor with four men under him. One will organise the day-to-day running of the hospital, the second will arrange the food, the third will look after the furniture and clothing, and the fourth will be in charge of the doctors.'

The official was lost for words. Nurse Nightingale knew how to get things done!

Despite all that Florence and her nurses did, 3,000 soldiers died in battle and a further 20,000 died of their injuries. That gave her much to think about, and Nurse Nightingale thought hard. Because of the detailed notes she always kept, she was full of ideas for improving army medical services. One of them was to open an Army Medical School, and she pushed and nagged until that happened. It took its first batch of students in 1860.

Soon after returning from the war, Florence became an invalid herself and spent most of her time in bed. That didn't stop her planning a better nursing service. Nor did it prevent her writing things down in one of her hundreds of notebooks.

Florence Nightingale

'The first thing a nurse should think about is her patients,' she wrote. 'And the second is their need of fresh air. They should be able to see out the window, to hear friendly voices, to have peace from unfamiliar noises.'

'What else would you suggest?' a colleague who was visiting her asked, after reading her notes.

Florence pulled herself up in bed.

'Patients should have flowers round about them, food when they are able to take it, comfortable pillows supporting them. Hospitals should be kept as clean as humanly possible ... and patients' skin should be washed and dried carefully to prevent sores.'

'I think you should have a rest,' the visitor said.

Florence's eyes were closed, but she continued speaking.

'Nurses should wash their hands often. They should learn to watch every little detail...'

'She never stops,' the visitor said, as she left Florence's room.

'We should thank God for that,' the woman with her commented. 'Florence Nightingale's non-stop work has changed nursing amazingly, especially the nursing of soldiers.

Factfile: *Nursing.* Before Florence's efforts nurses were not well trained or highly regarded. Healthcare in Britain at that time was not very advanced, and hospitals were dirty and often dangerous places. Florence helped to change this situation after her return from the Crimea. Other nursing schools were modelled on the one that she founded, and the Royal College of Nursing was founded in 1916. Registration of nurses was introduced in 1919. This meant that nurses received a standard training. Now many nurses train in universities and qualify with a degree in nursing.

Keynote: Florence encountered a good deal of disapproval and resistance to her attempts to reform nursing. Even some of the army officials did not approve of her efforts, but she pressed on. Florence believed that God had called her to be useful and to try and help others. She was able to press on because she realised that serving God and helping people

Florence Nightingale

was more important than making sure that important people liked her.

 Think: Florence found that she actually enjoyed helping people. When she was sad after the death of her cousin, she threw herself into trying to help people rather than brooding. It is easy to think that we only enjoy ourselves when we aren't thinking about anyone else, but that is not really the case. Think about some of the times that you have been able to help people. You will probably find that you actually enjoyed what you had to do for others.

 Prayer: Lord Jesus, thankyou for your example in working to help people and not being lazy. Thankyou for the satisfaction that I can get from trying to do good for other people. Please help me to see the needs of others and to develop a social conscience just as Florence did. Please help those who aren't as well off as I am. Amen.

Lottie Moon

Lottie sat on the back step of her lovely home in Virginia, her cousin Sarah at her side.

'I just can't imagine living anywhere else but here,' said ten-year-old Lottie. 'It's the most beautiful place in the whole wide world.'

Sarah, looking around, agreed. 'I'm going to miss the plantation when we go to Jerusalem. There won't be servants there to do everything for us, and there won't be slaves to do the outside work either.'

In the distance Lottie could see two slaves working. She wondered why her uncle was giving all this up to be a missionary.

'Do you really want to go?' she asked her cousin.

'I really do,' said Sarah. 'All of us do.'

Grabbing a handful of pea pods crossly, Lottie tried not to cry.

'Well I don't know why,' she complained. 'The Bible is just a story book, and it's a long way from Virginia to Jerusalem just to tell people fairy stories.'

Sarah looked sad. 'It's silly to say that.'

'It is not,' spat Lottie. 'It's missionaries that are silly, not me!'

When Sarah left for home that day, Lottie went to look for her older sister. She knew Orie would understand, for she didn't believe in God either.

'I hate when people go away,' Lottie told her father, three years later. 'Do you really have to go?'

Mr Moon smiled at his daughter. 'I'm afraid I do,' he said 'But New Orleans is not on the other side of the world and I'll be back before you have time to miss me.'

Lottie knew that wasn't true, because she loved her father very much and missed him even if he was only away overnight.

Just six days later, an envelope was delivered to her home. It was edged in black, and Mrs Moon's hand shook as she slit it open. And in the minute it took her mother to read the letter, Lottie's life changed forever. Her father had been aboard a steamboat that went on fire. Although he jumped to safety, Mr Moon died soon afterwards of a heart attack. Lottie's mother wept and prayed, but the girl had nobody to pray to because she didn't believe in God.

In 1855, when she was 14 years old, Lottie went with her younger sister to Virginia Female Seminary to study. Sometimes Lottie could be very serious, but there was a mischievous side to her too.

'It's April Fools' Day tomorrow,' she remembered in her bed, when nearly everyone else was asleep. 'What could I do for that?'

She thought, and thought, and thought. Then she nearly laughed aloud. It seemed to her that the days were full of bells tolling. One chime told them it was time to get up, another that lessons were beginning, and another that dinner was ready. Lottie and her friends felt bells tolling ruled their lives.

'I know what I'll do,' she decided, slipping silently out of bed. Taking her rolled-up blankets with her, she left the room and went to the bottom of the bell tower. Then she climbed the belfry ladder, crossed the rafters and climbed up a second ladder to the big brass bell.

'Shh,' she said, to both herself and the bell, as she wrapped her blankets round the clapper so that, when the bell was rung to wake them at 6 am, there would be just the dullest of thuds. And that's what happened.

'Who was responsible for that little trick?' the girls were asked.

There was no point in denying it, for Lottie was the only one who had no blankets on her bed!

When she moved on to college in 1857, Lottie enjoyed much more freedom.

'Do you need help?' she would ask her friends, as they struggled with their languages. She had no trouble learning languages and, at the end of Lottie's first year, she was top of the class in Greek, French, Spanish and Italian!

'What does the D stand for in Lottie D. Moon?' one of her friends asked, as they walked to their French class.

'It stands for Devil,' Lottie laughed.

Her friend's eyes opened wide. 'Does it really?'

Lottie hooted with laughter. 'It would suit me,' she giggled. 'The only reason I ever go to church is to see the good-looking boys and to pick holes in the minister's sermons.'

Although she knew that was true, her friend was still not convinced that D stood for Devil. It didn't.

'What are you two talking about?' Lottie asked Kate and Laura.

The girls looked uncomfortable.

'We were discussing whether to go to the special services at the Baptist Church,' Kate admitted.

'I suppose I could give myself an 18th birthday treat and go along too,' teased Lottie. 'That could be quite a laugh.'

Her friends looked embarrassed and changed the subject. They were even more embarrassed when Lottie appeared at the first service, and took a seat right at the front of the church! And their faces were plum coloured by the time their friend had looked round the church for them and winked.

'I must be losing my touch,' Lottie thought, as the service went on. 'I've not wanted to burst out laughing once so far. What a waste of time!'

That night she tossed and turned, and turned and tossed.

'This pillow's too hard,' she thought, punching it into a new shape.

'I wish that dog would stop barking! It's keeping me awake.'

At last, deciding that she just wasn't going to get to sleep, she turned on her back and thought.

'I wonder if there is anything in Christianity. I stopped believing because I saw Christians arguing with each other when I was a little girl, but maybe that was a bit rash,' she reasoned. 'That's not really a logical reason for giving something up, I suppose. People might argue over a game, but that doesn't mean they should stop playing it for ever.'

By the following morning, Lottie had decided that she would become a Christian. As she knew there was an early-morning prayer meeting, she got up on time to go to it.

'What does *she* want?' asked Kate, who was there before her. 'I bet she's looking for trouble.'

But Lottie was not. She was looking for a Saviour, the Lord Jesus Christ. And by the end of the day she had found him. Lottie D (not for Devil) became a Christian.

After training to be teachers, Lottie and her friend Anna, opened a school for girls in Cartersville, Georgia. And while they were working there, God called them both to be missionaries in China. One of Lottie's sisters was already there.

'Getting to San Francisco is just about as big an adventure as the sea voyage,' Lottie thought as her train crossed America. 'I just can't believe we're travelling so fast. Someone told me the train is going at 22 miles per hour!'

But the next part of the journey was not so pleasant, as the new young missionary wasn't a good sailor. Her hand was very shaky as she wrote a description of a hurricane in her diary. What was written under that was steadier. 'I can see the coast of China at last. Tomorrow, 7th October 1873, I will set foot on China for the very first time. I can hardly wait!'

Before she had been in China very long, Lottie was helping her sister run a school there. But something was bothering Lottie.

'I can't bear to look at the women's tiny feet,' she told her sister, Eddie. 'How do they make them so small?'

'Girls have their toes bent and tied under their feet until the bones break, when they are four or five years old. After that has happened, their toes can be turned back towards their ankles. They are then bound tightly to stop them from growing any bigger.'

Looking at a girl who was staggering along the road, it was obvious to Lottie that she was in great pain.

Eddie shook her head. 'Some girls can't walk for months when their feet are first bound. And none can run or skip ever again. But that's not the worst of it.'

Lottie wondered what could be worse than that.

'Some girls develop infections and eventually lose their legs. None recover from that. They all die.'

The smell of the market they were walking in had been making Lottie feel squeamish, but the thought of what Chinese girls went through made her feel thoroughly sick.

'What are they saying?' the new missionary asked her sister.

Eddie translated. 'They want to know if you are married, how many children you have, and why your mother-in-law lets you go out.'

'I don't have a mother-in-law!' Lottie protested. 'It's not their business anyway. And can you tell those girls to stop pawing me.'

A teenager was running her hand through Lottie's ringlets and two smaller girls stroked her silk dress with their very grubby fingers.

'You are going to have to learn to put up with that,' Eddie warned. 'And worse too.'

'Worse?' queried her sister.

'You'll have to get used to being called Foreign Devil and other such nasty names.'

Lottie had a sudden flashback to her college days. 'Is Lottie, D for Devil, Moon coming back to plague me?' she wondered.

Eddie became unwell and Lottie took her back to America. When Lottie returned to China, her dream was to open a school for girls.

'Why girls?' she was asked. 'They don't need to be educated to get married and have children.'

That kind of thinking really upset the missionary.

'Education will help free the girls,' she argued. 'At the moment they're not allowed to make any choices, everything is decided for them. They can't decide not to have their feet bound, but if they are educated they'll be able to choose to let their daughters run and jump and skip with normal comfortable feet. Girls who are educated will educate their daughters and things will be different for them.'

'You want to open a school here in Tengtchow?' she was asked.

Lottie said that was right.

Lottie Moon

'Well,' commented her companion. 'I don't think any girls will come.'

She could not have been more wrong. By the end of the school's first year, Lottie had 13 pupils. Because nobody would pay to have a girl educated, the missionary had to pay all the expenses for the girls: food, medicine, and accommodation. But she knew it was worth it.

In the winter of 1878, Lottie and another missionary went on a trip deep into the Chinese countryside to visit remote villages. They got such a welcome that they were able to tell many people about the Lord Jesus. She had prayed a lot about her disgust at dirt and smells, and about people touching her and asking personal questions. And on this trip, Lottie discovered that God had taken away her disgust. She just loved being with the villagers. In the years that followed, she had many trips to village communities, and saw a number of people become Christians.

'I go south to P'ingtu next week,' Lottie told a new missionary. 'No white woman has been there before.'

'How will you get the people to accept you?' she was asked.

'I have my secret weapon,' smiled Lottie. 'Sugar cookies!'

As soon as she set up home in P'ingtu,

the missionary baked some sugar cookies.
Little boys who came to the door were first
to try them. They liked them so much that
they told the villagers about the strange
sweet food. Others came to her door, adults
as well as children, and before long Lottie's
sugar cookies had won her many friends.
When the weather in P'ingtu grew so cold
she couldn't stop shivering despite wearing
all her clothes at once, Lottie Moon had
some Chinese clothes made for her. The
villagers liked her even more for that, and
because they liked her they listened to her
stories of Jesus.

'We have come on behalf of Dan Ho-
bang,' said one of three men who came to
her house. 'He wants you to go to our village
and tell us about Jesus.'

Lottie went with the men and discovered
that many people really wanted to know God's
good news. Crowds came to Dan Ho-bang's
house to hear what she had to say. To Lottie's
delight that was the beginning of a new and
lively church.

It became difficult for Christians in
China at the end of the 19th Century, and
many thousands were killed. Dan Ho-bang
was treated terribly. When Lottie heard
that a crowd was beating him, she yelled
above the noise.

Lottie Moon

'If you try to destroy the church here and the Christians who worship in it, you will have to kill me first. Our Master, Jesus, gave his life for us Christians, and now I am ready to die for him.'

'Then you will die, Foreign Devil,' a young man screamed, lifting a huge sword to strike Lottie down.

Suddenly his arm dropped and the sword clanged to the ground. God had stopped him from killing the missionary. The crowd, confused by what they had seen, melted away.

'Let me help you,' Lottie said, lifting Dan Ho-bang to his feet and taking him back to his home.

'The white woman does the things that her Jesus did,' people said, who listened to Lottie and watched how she lived. And they were able to watch her as she grew old too, because she remained in China until 1912, and died on the ship as she travelled home to America.

Fact File: *The Boxer Uprising.* Much of the persecution of Christians in China at the end of the 19th century was due to a movement known as the Boxer Uprising. Big defeats in the European wars led to a lot of resentment of foreigners in China. The dowager empress of China allowed the growth of a secret, anti-foreign society known as the Boxers (or Righteous Fists). In 1899 they began to attack foreigners and Chinese Christians, whom they felt had adopted the religion of foreigners. In 1900 they besieged the Chinese capital, but this siege was eventually broken. Many Christians, both Chinese and foreign, were killed during the Boxer Uprising.

 Keynote: Lottie was willing to go deep into China, even to places where no white woman had gone before, to tell people about Jesus. She was even willing to bake sugar cookies for them so that they would listen to her! The trip was dangerous and she was in an unknown country where she didn't know anybody. Lottie was willing to do all of this because she realised that Jesus had come to save Chinese people just as much as white people.

Think: When Lottie was young, she didn't take Christianity very seriously at all, and she was annoyed when her uncle decided to go off to Jerusalem to be a missionary. She had written off Christianity because she had seen Christians arguing. She later realised that this did not really disprove the faith. Can you think of any other things that are true but people still argue about?

Prayer: Lord Jesus, thankyou for the good news about what you did to save people from their sins. Thankyou that we can believe it and know that it is true. Thankyou for people who travel all over the world to tell people about you and for those who tell their next-door neighbours too. Please help everyone who tries to tell someone else about you today. Amen.

Ida Scudder

The eight girls in Dorm 3 raced to their beds, jumped in, pulled their blankets up to their chins and smiled sweetly when their teacher came in.

'Everyone tucked up and ready to sleep?' Miss Tomkins asked.

'Yes, Miss,' eight voices replied in unison.

'Goodnight, girls,' their teacher said.

'Goodnight, Miss Tomkins,' answered the girls sleepily.

But when the door clicked behind Miss Tomkins, all eight sat up in bed, as wide-awake as could be.

'What are we going to discuss tonight?' Florence asked.

'Let's talk about being grown up,' suggested Mary. 'That always gives me something nice to dream about.'

Ida laughed quietly. 'We'll have to watch what we say or we'll give Mary nightmares!'

'What do you want to be, Ida?' Mary asked. 'And make it something nice.'

Ida lay back on her pillow. 'I'd like to marry a rich and handsome man then I wouldn't have to work. I'd stay in bed until lunchtime each day reading and drinking coffee. Some afternoons I'd play tennis, and others I'd go driving. And there would be a party to go to every single evening. Most nights we'd not get home till about 3am, which is why I'd stay in bed till lunchtime.'

Florence giggled. 'I'm quite sure that dream won't come true.'

'Why not?' Ida demanded.

'Because you'll be a missionary like your parents, and that means you'll be poor and up early every morning. The only parties you'll get to are babies' birthday parties!'

Ida sat up crossly. 'I won't be a missionary!' she raged. 'I won't!'

Florence was sorry she'd upset her friend, so she tried to change the subject.

'What will you do when you grow up?' she asked the girl in the next bed.

Mary sighed dreamily. 'I think I might like to be a missionary,' she said. 'African and Indian children are so cute, and it would be warm in these faraway places. The food is exotic and the clothes are so elegant. I can just see myself in a shimmering gold sari.'

Ida sat up in bed. She'd heard quite enough nonsense and felt it was time to tell her friends what it was really like in India.

'It's not exotic at all,' she began. 'And the weather is much better here in America. In India it is either so hot that absolutely everything is covered in dust, or so wet that everything is drowned in mud.'

'Ugh!' said Mary. 'Maybe I'll stay right here.'

'And as for babies' birthday parties,' Ida went on, 'when I was just six years old I had to feed children that were dying of starvation. They were so weak I had to break the bread into crumbs and put it into their mouths.' She shuddered at the memory. 'I've even seen dead bodies lying in the streets.'

'That decides it,' Mary announced. 'Whatever I do, I'll not be a missionary.'

'And nor will I,' said Ida. 'I definitely won't!'

Florence shushed her friends. 'Tuck up!' she whispered. 'I think I can hear Miss Tomkins!'

When the time came for the girls to leave school, Ida's mother was ill and needed her help.

'I've got to go back to India to help Mum,' she told Florence. 'But as soon as she's better I'll be heading right home to America.'

'I'll write to you,' her friend promised. 'And I'll tell you all the fun things we're doing.'

So Ida found herself back in South India. She nursed her mother well, mostly because she wanted her to get better, but also because she wanted to leave India as quickly as she possibly could.

'Is that another letter from Florence?' Mrs Scudder asked Ida one day.

Her daughter nodded and took the letter to her room to read it in peace.

Ida felt so homesick for America as she read her friend's news of parties and picnics and boyfriends. And she was feeling sorry for herself when she heard footsteps outside on the veranda. When Ida went out, she found a tall Brahmin man there.

'Amma,' he said, bowing his head and holding his hands together, 'please come and help my wife.'

'What's wrong with her?' Ida asked.

'She is having a baby and things are not well with her.'

'I'll get my father,' Ida told the man. 'He'll be able to help because he's a doctor.'

The Brahmin shook his head. 'It needs to be a woman,' he said. 'My religion won't allow a male doctor to see a female patient.'

Ida explained that she knew nothing about medicine and couldn't help.

That same night two other men came to ask her to help their young wives. In the morning, Ida heard that these three young women had all died because there wasn't a woman doctor to help them have their babies. Ida did some very hard thinking that sad morning, and she realised that God had to come first in her life, above friends and parties and everything else. And she knew what she had to do with her life. Ida went looking for her parents.

'I have something to tell you,' she announced, when she found them. 'I want to go back to America to study medicine then I'll come and help the poor women who are not allowed to see a male doctor.'

On 1st January 1900, Dr Ida Scudder arrived back in India. She was so excited at the prospect of seeing her parents again. But sad news was waiting for her.

'Your father's very ill,' she was told, 'and nothing seems to be helping him.'

Although the new young doctor did all she could, her father's condition grew worse.

'I can't work on my own,' she worried. 'I thought Dad would be here to help me.'

'Even if I do recover,' her father told Ida, 'it will be a long time before I'm fit to work again. So I think you should make a start with the women.'

Ida felt that things were working out very badly. She prayed about what she should do and felt that God was showing her that her father was right. Doctor Ida set up a tiny clinic in the mission house that had been her childhood home, and within an amazingly short time poor women heard that she was willing to treat them and came to the clinic. Wealthier women also wanted her help, but they expected her to visit them in their homes.

Just five months after Ida arrived back in India, her father died.

'How am I going to cope with doing operations without Dad's advice?' she asked herself, over and over again.

But the day came when she had no choice but to perform a big operation on a very ill woman. When she had finished the surgery, Ida paced the veranda, not knowing if the woman would get better or die. But within two days her patient was sitting up in bed and doing very well. Ida thanked God from the bottom of her heart and did a further two operations almost immediately. Young Doctor Scudder very quickly became well known, and before long her work outgrew the mission bungalow and a hospital was built. She had taken money from America to build a hospital at Vellore, but an outbreak of plague meant that it wasn't completed until 1902.

Ida Scudder

Doctor-Amma (that's what Ida was known as) worked hard to make the hospital as good as it could possibly be, and the nurses and other staff did too. Patients came from many miles away, almost all of them women who would not otherwise have got medical help at all, as the only other doctors were men. Many, many women who would have died had the hospital not been there, recovered from their illnesses and told all their friends about Doctor-Amma.

'We can't take on any more work,' the nursing sister told Ida one day. 'Between the hospital and your road-side clinics the staff are worked off their feet.'

Dr Scudder nodded in agreement. 'We need more staff,' she said, 'and not only nurses. We need more doctors too.'

'Would some come from America, or perhaps Britain, to help?' Sister asked.

'I don't think there's any chance of that,' Doctor-Amma said slowly ... something was buzzing round in her mind. 'Was this the time to tell Sister what she'd been thinking about for a long time?' Ida wondered. She decided it was.

'We've been training our own nurses for several years, could we not train our own doctors?' she asked.

The Sister, who had been folding a sheet,

stopped what she was doing and looked at her friend. 'You're not serious, are you?'

But Ida Scudder had never been more serious in her life.

For the following five years Ida discussed the possibility with people who knew about medical training, and with the Surgeon-General in Madras. Eventually, in 1918, she got his permission to open a Christian medical school for girls, even though he made it quite clear he thought she wouldn't get any students, and even if she did, they wouldn't make it to be doctors. Ida advertised the course, and out of those who applied she chose her first class of students. Before they arrived to begin their studies, Doctor-Amma arranged the building of a shed for dissections, hired a hall for lectures, and bought books, a microscope and a skeleton.

'Doctor-Amma is like a hen with chickens,' Sister told her friend Ruth, some time after the medical school was up and running. 'Everywhere she goes she has this trail of students behind her. She does most of the lecturing herself, though the other doctors help, and they go on all her ward rounds with her. She takes hardly any time off.'

Ruth looked surprised. 'Does she teach them in the evenings too?' she asked.

Ida Scudder

'No,' Sister smiled. 'She plays tennis and basketball with them, or takes them out in that car of hers.'

'She sounds more of a friend than a college principal,' Ruth suggested.

Sister laughed. 'Because she relaxes with them doesn't mean they get off lightly in their work. Let me tell you a story Ida told me just the other day.'

Sipping her tea, Ruth listened.

'It happened on a day when the locals were on holiday. When Doctor-Amma went into the lecture hall, one of the students asked if they might have a holiday too. Ida demanded to know why they should have a holiday when she'd been up till two in the morning preparing a lecture for them. She was so cross that she walked out of the lecture hall, banging the door behind her. A few hours later, the student who had asked for the holiday arrived at the hospital with flowers for Ida, and to explain they had wanted the day off to revise for an exam!'

'What did Doctor-Amma say to that?' Ruth asked.

Sister grinned. 'She was so ashamed at having given them a row, she let them have the afternoon off to study and prepared a tea-party to celebrate the holiday!'

The two women walked along the road towards the hospital.

'With all the girls being Christians they'll no doubt forgive Doctor-Amma for her impatience,' said Ruth.

Sister looked at her. 'What makes you think they are all Christians?' she asked.

'I assumed they were because it's a Christian medical college.'

'Not at all,' her friend explained. 'Ida chose the cleverest students, not just the Christian ones. We have Hindu and Muslim girls as well. Of course, Ida prays for them and tells them about the Lord Jesus as well as about infectious diseases.'

It took several years to teach the girls all they needed to know to be doctors, but eventually the great day came when they took their final examinations. They sat the exam, not at the hospital, but at the university with all the other medical students. It was an anxious wait for the results. And when they came, the male students heard first.

'Only one in every five of them passed,' a university official told Ida.

The students overheard. 'That would mean only two out of the fourteen of us would pass,' she said to her friend.

Doctor-Amma looked sympathetic as the thought passed through her mind that none

Ida Scudder

of them might pass at all. Eventually she was called into the office to be told the results.

'Here she comes,' one of her students whispered, as the office door opened.

'You've passed!' Ida told the girls. 'You've passed! Every one of you! Not only that, but four of you got First Class degrees and another two won gold medals!'

The fourteen new young doctors hugged and kissed each other in their excitement, and in the midst of the huddle was Ida Scudder, who was every bit as delighted as they were.

Ida Scudder retired in 1946, aged 75, though she continued advising on difficult patients and teaching a weekly Bible Class for ten years after that. When she retired, one of her own students took over her work. Ida's first clinic had just one bed, but she lived to see the building of the Vellore Christian Medical School and College, with nearly 500 beds, 100 doctors, its own nursing school, and a college taking 200 new medical students each year.

Fact File: *India.* Ida's parents were medical missionaries in India. India is a subcontinent southwest of China. When they were there, India was part of the British Empire. Parts of India were very poor indeed and were troubled by lack of food and proper medical care. When India became independent from Britain in 1947, the northern (and mainly Muslim) part was separated to form Pakistan. There are still problems with diseases such as leprosy and cholera in parts of India, and several aid agencies carry out a good deal of their work there.

Keynote: Ida knew what it meant to be a missionary in India because she had seen what her parents did. She did not have any of the romantic notions that some of her friends had. When she was a little girl, Ida knew that it would not be easy, and did not want to be a missionary. But she went there all the same when she saw the need and felt God's call. Although the things that we are asked to do are not always pleasant at first, we will usually find, as Ida did, that they are worthwhile in the long run.

Think: There was a world of difference between the life that Ida led when she was in America with her friends, and that which she led in India but God watched over her in both places. God knows us and can see us wherever we are in the world. He is able to care for us even when he asks us to go to far away places that are different from anything that we know. When were you furthest from your home? What did it feel like?

Prayer: Lord Jesus, thank you for the way you helped sick people when you lived on earth, and the way you care for us today. Please bless missionary doctors who are willing to go and help the sick and suffering in faraway lands. Help me to be willing to do what you want me to do in my life.
Amen.

Jeanette Li

When Mooi Nga* was five years old, she saw a big boy hurt a girl much younger than himself. Mooi Nga was furious! She punched the boy and, when he swore at her, she swore back. Mooi Nga's father passed along the road just as the fight took place.

'Mooi Nga, come here!' he called.

The child ran to his side, expecting her usual hug. Instead he marched her home and told his wife to punish her!

'That kind of behaviour is a disgrace to the family, and in public too!' he said crossly. 'Don't you ever do anything like that again!'

When her father thought she had been punished enough, he took the child out into the garden.

'Your name, Mooi Nga, means Jasmine Bud,' he told her. 'And that's a beautiful thing. When you were born your mother thought that might tempt evil spirits to harm you, that's why she calls you Ch'ao Nga which means ugly cry-baby.'

*At home Jeanette was called Mooi Nga. Her English name is Jeanette Li.

'Tell me about when I was born,' the girl asked.

Her father sighed deeply. 'When the midwife saw you were a girl, she wanted me to put you in an orphanage. But your mother and I couldn't do that. Even though you weren't a boy you were precious to us, you were still a gift from the Buddha.'

Mooi Nga often thought back to that conversation, especially the following year, when life seemed to crash about her.

'What does it mean to be dead?' she asked her mother.

The poor woman's husband had just died, and she couldn't explain to her two little daughters that they would never see their father again.

'He's gone to be with the ancestors,' she said.

Even when Mooi Nga saw her father in his coffin, she could not take in that he had gone forever. Not only did the girl lose her father, very soon she lost her sister too. Her mother was tricked into giving her sister away in order to repay her father's debts.

Two years later, when Mooi Nga was eight years old, she suddenly became seriously ill.

'Take her to the Mission Hospital,' a relative said to her mother.

But her mother was too scared to do that.

'I've heard that they take children's eyeballs out,' she said fearfully. 'And I won't let them do that to my daughter.'

But Mooi Nga grew worse, and eventually she was taken to the hospital where she was treated very well.

'Father! Where are you?' she called out all night in her fever.

'Your heavenly Father is with you,' the missionaries told her. 'He won't leave you.'

But the little girl did not want a heavenly Father, she wanted her dad back again. However, as the kind missionaries told her about God she discovered that she did want a heavenly Father after all, and that she wanted the Lord Jesus to be her Saviour. By the time she was well, Mooi Nga was a Christian. Both she and her mother were baptised not long afterwards, and then she became a pupil in the mission school.

It was 1915, and Mooi Nga was about to be married.

'I want to study,' she told her mother, 'not cook and clean for my husband and mother-in-law.'

'You have been promised to Lei Wing Kan since you were nine years old,' she was told. 'It is now time you were married.'

Although the girl argued her case loudly and strongly the marriage still went ahead. She and her husband were both the same age; they were just fifteen. In the next few years they had a son and a daughter. Sadly, their little girl died. Eventually Lei Wing Kan went off to study and left his wife behind. They never lived together again and Mooi Nga brought up her son, called Min Ch'iu, as a single mother. Her job as a teacher gave them enough money to live on.

When Min Ch'iu was twelve years old, his mother became a student at Bible School.

'God has put it in my heart to be a missionary right here at home to my own Chinese people,' Mooi Nga explained to him.

So in 1931 they moved to Chagsha, and to Bible School. Three years later, newly qualified as a Bible woman, Mooi Nga prepared to go to the Black Dragon Province of Manchuria, and her son went into boarding school to finish his education. She sent him a letter shortly after she arrived.

'I boarded the train at Nanking on 24th August,' she wrote, 'and travelled the thousand miles to my new home. A missionary was on the platform waiting for me when I arrived. There are two lady missionaries here, and I will be working with them. We soon found a suitable house. But when we moved in we discovered we were not the only residents. On the first night I woke up with something crawling over my face. I turned on a light and saw cockroaches everywhere! The walls were thick with them. The next day we cemented all the cracks we could find and hoped that would stop them coming in. But we were woken by the tapping of hundreds of tiny cockroach-feet! Eventually we got rid of the cockroaches ... only to be overrun with mice and rats. Now that we've trapped the last of them, we'll get on with our work for the Lord.'

Three months later, Mooi Nga wrote to her son again, this time with news of her first trip into the country.

'When we arrived in Mengshui, we made a procession around the town carrying a big poster announcing our meetings. One person carried the poster, another gave out leaflets about the Lord Jesus, and I rang a bell to attract people's attention. By the time we held our open-air service quite a crowd had gathered around us. And at the end an old Christian man introduced himself and invited us to his home.'

But when she wrote at Christmas time, her letter painted quite a different picture.

'In Mengshui we rented a building large enough for over a hundred people. Because it had been empty for two years, draughts came in everywhere. Although there was a fire, it was impossible to keep warm. It was so cold that the tea we had left in the teapot froze and cracked the teapot! We are to be here till February next year, so please pray that your poor mother doesn't freeze to death.'

'What's the name of the man who comes round the doors selling things?' Mooi Nga asked her neighbour.

'He is Mr Wang,' she was told, 'and he sells jewellery, toys, kitchen idols and images of Buddha.'

The missionaries took every opportunity to tell Mr Wang about Jesus, and eventually he became a Christian.

'I don't know what to do,' he told Mooi Nga soon afterwards. 'I have a stock of idols and Buddhas still to sell, and I can't afford just to destroy them.'

'A Christian can't sell idols,' he was told. 'God would not like that.'

Over the next week or two Mr Wang's sales went right down until he wasn't earning enough to keep his family. One night he heard a sermon that showed him what the problem was. He hadn't destroyed the idols, and God was not pleased with him.

'I'm going right home to destroy them all,' he told his friends at church. He did just that, and the following day people started buying things from him again.

In the spring of 1940, Mooi Nga moved to Taikang. Unsure of how to begin her work there, God showed her she should first work with children. 'But how can I interest them?' she wondered.

Just then a cart of grass was driven along the road, and she noticed children darting out and stealing grass off the cart.

'Excuse me!' she called to the man whose cart it was. 'If I pay for the grass the children have stolen, will you promise not to get them into trouble?'

The man agreed, and told her to take the boys and girls away and teach them not to steal. Very soon she had a lively children's club. Not only did the children stop stealing, but they also learned about Jesus.

During the Second World War there was also a war between China and Japan. The Japanese occupied Manchuria, the area in which Mooi Nga worked.

'The Emperor of Japan has passed a law saying that every home must have a shrine, a god-shelf, at which they are to worship the Emperor idols.'

'Every home!' declared Mooi Nga. 'There won't be idols in my home! And I most certainly won't be worshipping the Emperor of Japan!'

One day an official came to see if the missionary was keeping the law.

'I will only worship the Lord God,' she told him, showing him where in the Bible it said idols should not be worshipped.

'Do you worship your ancestors?' the man asked.

'No,' Mooi Nga explained. 'I only worship the one true God.'

From then on she was watched very closely and with great suspicion. Friends of hers were arrested as prisoners of war. Although things became very difficult and dangerous, Mooi Nga continued her missionary work and did good even to those who were determined to harm her.

By 1948 most countries were beginning to recover after the Second World War, but China was going from bad to worse. The Communists had taken over the country, and people were terribly oppressed. Mooi Nga went back to her home area of Tak Hing, where she was asked to take over the running of an orphanage.

'Why should I do that?' she asked. 'My job is to tell people about Jesus.'

'We believe you are the right person,' she was told.

And after she had prayed about it, the missionary decided they were right. Her work changed completely, as she found herself in charge of an orphanage full of needy children.

'What age of children do you have to care for?' Mooi Nga's son asked, in a letter.

'We have both boys and girls,' she replied, 'and they are from a few months old to 14 or 15. One of the first things I did when I came here was get some good cats to catch the rats. But they were so good the Communists stole them!'

Rats were not Mooi Nga's only problem. The orphanage had been run badly, and she set out to improve it.

'We have 64 children here,' she told her helper, 'so we need to divide them into groups, each group with an older person in charge. And we need to encourage the children to work and study. If they are busy they'll be less aware of the troubled time we are living in, and of the dangers all around us.'

But Mooi Nga could not protect the children from the Communists, because they were all around. Nor could she protect herself.

'There are some people looking for you,' the water-carrier told her, one morning.

'What do they want?' she asked.

The old man did not know.

Mooi Nga didn't go to look for the visitors as it was Sunday, and the service was just about to begin. They found her afterwards, and told her she was under arrest.

How glad the orphanage staff were to see her back late that night. But Mooi Nga knew that she would be arrested again, and that she would not get out in a day next time.

The People's Government of Communist China declared that there was no God. Those who were 'foolish' enough to think that God did exist were required to register with their local authorities. A law passed in 1950 limited what Christians could do, and made mission work illegal. The Red Army ruled the country and everyone, from the richest to the poorest, was closely controlled. Christians were constantly spied on and always in danger.

The following year, while Mooi Nga was working in the church garden, more than 60 men entered the church and the orphanage.

'Give us the keys to all the rooms, chests, drawers, and desks,' they demanded.

She gave them what they wanted

'What are you doing?' Mooi Nga asked,

as the men sealed each door with an official seal.

A soldier stared her in the eye. 'The People's Government of China is taking over the orphanage and church,' he said, in his bossiest voice.

The missionary continued to work at the orphanage under a Communist overseer. It saddened her terribly when the older children were sent out to beg or to spy.

Over the years that followed, Mooi Nga was imprisoned several times; she was even brainwashed. Following her release in 1953 she moved to Canton, then later made her home in Hong Kong, where she continued in mission work. By then her son and his family had made their home in the United States, and in 1962 she joined them there. Mooi Nga's heart was always with her beloved people in China, to many of whom she had given a hope and a future when life was unspeakably difficult.

Fact File: *The Cultural Revolution.* The Communists took control of China in 1948 in a revolution, which sought to overturn many of the traditional Chinese practices, and make it impossible ever to return to capitalism. People from universities were forced to work in the fields, and many private businesses and organisations like the orphanage were seized. Children in schools were forced to read the writings of the Communist leader. China is one of the few countries in the world that still maintains a Communist system of government although it has been trying to engage more and more with the outside world in recent years.

Keynote: Mooi Nga wanted her dad when she was ill and feverish in the Mission Hospital, and the thought of a heavenly Father did not cheer her up much. Before she left the hospital, however, she had discovered her need of her heavenly Father, and she went on to tell lots of other people about God so that they could know their heavenly Father too. The missionaries had said that he would never leave her, and he didn't, even in the dark days of the Japanese invasion and the Cultural Revolution.

 Think: Mooi Nga's mother was scared to take her to the Mission Hospital because she thought that they would gouge her eyes out. Of course, the missionaries were there to help the people not to hurt them. It might seem as if our parents and teachers are doing things just to take away all our fun but they do it for our good. We may even discover, as Mooi Nga did, that we learn things from them about Jesus that are far more amazing than anything that we could have imagined.

 Prayer: Lord Jesus, thankyou for being in control even in the dark and difficult times. Please help me to trust you even when things do not go as I would like them to. Thankyou for the people who continued to trust in you even through the Cultural Revolution. Please be with all those who are suffering because they trust in you today. Amen.

Henrietta Mears

Elizabeth pulled the long red gown over her head, and thrust her arms down its sleeves.

'You'll have to roll up the sleeves,' Henrietta told her, 'or you'll not be able to eat your cookies.'

The two girls giggled. Henrietta had on a black velvet dress that went down to the ground then wrapped itself round her feet. Over that she wore a lacy stole. And on top of the miniature fashion statement was a hat, and what a hat!

'Did your mum ever wear that hat?' Elizabeth asked, trying hard not to laugh.

Henrietta managed to get to the full-length mirror without tripping over the crumpled velvet at her feet. Standing in front of it, she gave a report on herself of the kind that was sometimes in the Minnesota newspapers.

'Miss Henrietta Mears from Duluth was present at the function,' she said, in her most grown-up and official voice. 'She wore a shimmering dress of rich black velvet, topped with a hand-made lace stole. Her hat, created by the designer Blah-di-Blah, was a confection of delicate lace flowers and bird feathers. An ostrich feather, dyed a delightful shade of powder blue, wrapped itself round the brim and reached out to tickle the neck of her escort. Miss Mears' gold rimmed spectacles glinted from underneath her splendid hat.'

Laughter tears streamed down Elizabeth's face as Henrietta turned round from the mirror, and they both dissolved in giggles when she tripped over the tail of her dress and landed on the bed beside her friend. The confection of delicate lace flowers and bird feathers sailed off her head and landed on her doll's house.

As they packed the dressing-up clothes away the two girls worked carefully. The dresses were folded into a trunk, with camphor balls in between them to keep away the moths. Scarves, stoles and gloves were wrapped in tissue paper and placed in a drawer. They had just tidied things away when there was a knock at the door.

'Time for cookies,' Henrietta's sister Margaret said, smiling broadly, her head peering round the doorframe at the two youngsters.

'Have you been dressing up again?' she asked.

Henrietta said that they had.

'I don't know anyone else who has so many dressing-up clothes,' Elizabeth commented.

'That's because you don't know anyone else who has six brothers and sisters, and whose next sister up is eleven years older than her. Lots of these clothes were mine, but they are way out of fashion nowadays.'

Elizabeth looked puzzled. 'I didn't know you have six brothers and sisters,' she said to her friend.

'Two of them died and are in heaven with Jesus,' Henrietta explained.

'I love Easter!' Henrietta announced. 'It's one of my favourite times of the year.'

'Mine too,' said her mother. 'The day that reminds us about Jesus rising from the dead is very special indeed.'

The seven-year-old looked serious. 'That's because he died to save us from our sins,' she agreed. 'So that we can be forgiven and go to heaven, like my brother and sister.'

Mrs Mears was brushing Henrietta's long hair, when the girl turned round and looked at her mother seriously.

'I'm ready to become a Christian and join the church,' she said.

He mother stopped brushing. 'I'm afraid you're so young that some people might think you don't really understand.'

'But I do understand,' insisted the girl. 'I know I'm a sinner and I know Jesus is my Saviour. That means I'm ready to join the church.'

Wrapping her daughter's ringlets round her fingers, Mrs Mears suggested that they speak to their minister. A few weeks later Henrietta and her cousin, who was just the same age, stood at the front of the congregation and answered questions about their faith in the Lord Jesus. A week or two later, the girls were baptised and became members of the church.

'Why do we have to get up early even on Saturdays and holidays?' Henrietta asked her sister, at the end of the next school term.

'Mum doesn't like us wasting time,' Margaret said. 'Have you ever seen her waste a minute?'

Henrietta sat up in bed and thought.

'No,' she decided. 'If she has five minutes between doing things she plays the piano or reads a little bit of a book.' The girl giggled at something that came into her mind. 'Sometimes when I'm reading,' she said, 'Mum snaps my book shut and asks me what I've read, just to make sure I'm taking it in.'

'I know,' laughed Margaret. 'She used to do the same to me!'

That evening, before settling down to

sleep, Henrietta thought about her mother's life, and wrote down some things her mother did that she wanted to do too.

'I will never waste time,' she wrote. 'I will always read good books. I will help people in need. I will talk to others about Jesus. I will pray for others as well as for myself.'

'I'm not feeling very well,' Henrietta told her mother, one day.

'What's the matter with you?' she was asked.

'I ache all over and I have a headache,' the twelve-year-old explained.

'That sounds like flu,' Mrs Mears decided. 'Go to bed and you may feel better after a sleep.'

Henrietta went to bed and slept, but she felt worse when she woke up. In the days that followed her muscles grew stiff and sore, and her joints ached terribly. She had a raging fever and was very unwell. Mr and Mrs Mears sent for the doctor. After he had examined the girl, he looked most serious.

'I'm afraid the news is not good,' he told Mrs Mears. 'Henrietta has muscular rheumatism. Recovery is a long and slow process, and not everyone recovers.'

'You mean it can be fatal?'

'Your daughter's a strong girl,' the doctor said gently. 'But, yes, it can be.'

Mrs Mears put her head in her hands. For a second the doctor thought she was crying, but she was praying for the daughter she loved so much.

Henrietta's condition grew worse over the weeks and months that followed, until she was hardly able to move at all.

'Some other children in the area have the same thing,' the doctor told Mrs Mears, when he visited. 'One of them is critically ill.'

'Who is that?' the woman asked.

When the doctor told her the girl's name, Mrs Mears recognised it as Henrietta's good friend. She died shortly afterwards.

As well as suffering from muscular rheumatism, Henrietta began having very serious nosebleeds. An elder from her church came and prayed for her, and they stopped right away, though her rheumatism remained the same. Henrietta could not walk more than a few steps for nearly two years. It was as though she was stuck in one position, and she wondered if she would be like that for the rest of her life. When friends came to visit her, Henrietta was laid on a little bed near the garden where she could talk to them and watch them playing their games.

'My legs can't run and jump now,' she told them. 'But my heart can still dance.'

Eventually, when the girl was 14 years

old, the elder came back and prayed with her again. God answered their prayers and Henrietta immediately began to recover.

'I've learned a lot in these two years,' she told her sister. 'I've especially learned to trust my future to God, and not to fret about it. But that doesn't stop me wondering what he has in store for me.'

Margaret looked at the frail teenager, and wondered the same thing.

A further challenge faced Henrietta when she started studying at the University of Minnesota. She had always worn spectacles, but she noticed that her eyesight was getting worse.

'You have a choice,' the eye specialist told her. 'You can give up reading and keep your eyesight, or you can continue reading and studying and be blind by the time you are 30.'

Henrietta thought long and hard about that, and prayed over it too.

'If I'm going to be blind by the time I'm 30,' she decided, 'then blind I shall be! But I'll want something in my head to think about, so I'm going to study as hard as I can for as long as I can.'

And that's what she did. After doing very well at university, she became a school teacher and Sunday school teacher too.

'I really need your help,' Margaret Mears

said. 'The girls in my Sunday school class call themselves The Snobs. They won't let anyone else join the class, and they won't listen to me either!'

Henrietta took over the class, and the girls changed a lot. Two of them even went round the neighbourhood inviting other girls in! One week later, 55 girls turned up, and within ten years Henrietta's class numbered over 500! A special hall had to be built for them.

'What hat will Teacher have on today?' the girls used to ask. 'Will it have ostrich feathers or wax grapes on it?'

Henrietta was popular, and her amazing collection of hats became famous!

Henrietta Mears' 30th birthday came and went, and much to her delight her eyesight did not fail. It seemed that she was not becoming blind after all.

In 1928, when Henrietta was 38 years old, she and her sister Margaret moved to Hollywood. She had accepted a job as Director of Christian Education at the First Presbyterian Church of Hollywood. When she arrived, there were 450 students, two-and-a-half years later the number had grown to 4,200.

'How does she do it?' people asked.

One man who knew her well answered the question. 'She trusts in God and expects him to do great things. When Henrietta prays, she really expects answers. As soon as she opens her eyes, she looks around to see what the answer is.'

'You want us to write our own Sunday school books!' one of her teachers said. 'What's wrong with the ones we use at present?'

Henrietta explained that she had been unable to find teaching books that really taught what the Bible said.

'Most of them seem to be written by people who don't believe the Bible, and what's the use of teaching children that what the God of truth says is not always true? Do you know what a boy said to me the other day?' she asked the teacher. 'He told me he didn't want to go to Sunday school any more because he was told the same story over and over again and each time it just got dumber! We've got to make sure that doesn't happen here!'

That was the beginning of Henrietta writing Sunday school lessons, and it ended up as a publishing company that supplied books by the thousand! At the end of 1933, just five years after she went to Hollywood, she had 6,500 pupils in her Sunday school, and over 13,000 copies of her workbooks had been sold in 25 states of the USA. Gospel Press, as the company was called, grew to be very famous.

'It's grand having young people on Sundays,' Henrietta told her fellow teachers, 'but we want to take them off to camps too, so that we can have longer spells of time with them.'

'You mean conferences for the university students?' one asked.

'I mean good fun Bible holidays for anyone, clever or not!'

One campsite was found, then another, then a third, and many young people became Christians at them.

'I have a dream for a much bigger campsite,' Henrietta said to her sister Margaret.

'That's your motto, "Dream Big"', Margaret laughed.

'So it is!' agreed Henrietta, as she straightened her hat in the mirror. 'I like this one,' she added. 'The feathers along the side look really pretty.'

'I've heard about a place called Forest Home,' a friend told the Mears sisters. 'And I'm taking you to see it.'

They drove to view the beautiful house and estate.

'This is the most elegant place I've ever seen,' said Henrietta, 'but you can drive right past, because we can't possibly afford it.'

Henrietta Mears

'The place is worth $350,000,' their friend Bill explained. 'Let's try offering $50,000 and see what happens.'

The offer was put in and people were asked to pray about it. Months passed, then one day there was a tremendous thunderstorm near Forest Home. Trees crashed down, some cabins were destroyed. Hillsides were washed away but Forest Home and the campsite round about it escaped serious damage. In the calm after the storm Henrietta's telephone rang.

'It's Bill,' a voice said, at the end of the line. 'The son of the owner of Forest Home has offered to sell it to us for $30,000!'

A day or two later, when the announcement was made in church, Henrietta's hat was the most amazing celebration of colour. But it was nothing to the joy in her heart. She was dreaming big, and in her big dreams she saw many hundreds of young people becoming Christians at Forest Home. And because Henrietta's dreams were also her prayers, she saw them come true.

Fact File: *Hats.* Henrietta was well known for her collection of spectacular hats. In the 19th and early 20th centuries it was much more common for ladies to wear hats when they went out (and especially when they went to church) than it is today. Hats are still worn at certain social occasions like weddings. One of the best known in Britain is Royal Ascot, which is a series of horse races. Many women attend, often in very fancy and expensive hats.

Keynote: Henrietta saw her mother's good example and wanted to follow it. The good things Mrs Mears did she had learned from the Bible. Later on, Henrietta became a good example to those who saw her successes in Sunday school teaching. The Bible tells us that it is important that we encourage one another in faith by words and example. Trying to read good books, help people in need, tell others about Jesus, and pray for others as well as ourselves, are good ways to start doing this.

Henrietta Mears

 Think: After Henrietta went to the First Presbyterian Church of Hollywood, she decided that she needed to write her own material because the materials that they were using did not really teach what the Bible said. She realised how important it was to teach what the Bible actually said. The Bible tells us that God hears and answers the prayers of people who trust in him. Henrietta didn't just believe that, she acted on it. She was ambitious in what she tried to achieve for God, and she was successful because she did it prayerfully.

 Prayer: Lord Jesus, thankyou for living a life that was such a good example for all of us. Help me to follow your example, and that of those around me who obey you. Thankyou for the Bible and for all the amazing promises that it has for us. Please help me to really believe and trust when I pray to you. Amen.

Bessie Adams

An easterly wind blew along the English Channel, and it seemed to blow its way through Bessie. She ran to heat herself up, and arrived home puffed but reasonably warm.

'My,' said her mother, 'you're in a right hurry today.'

'I ran because I was shivering with cold,' the girl explained.

Mrs Miners took a long hard look at her daughter.

'That coat's too short and too tight,' she decided. 'The buttons hardly close on you. No wonder you're feeling the cold.'

'Do I need a new coat?' the eleven-year-old asked, knowing that coats cost money, and that with so many brothers and sisters there was not much of that to go round. Smiling at her daughter, Mrs Miners explained what she would do. 'You remember your sister's coat from two years ago?' she asked.

Bessie nodded.

'Well there's plenty of material in it to

make you a coat that will look quite different. I'll unpick all the seams and cut one to a new design. And I'll turn the material inside out so that it looks like new. Would you like navy trimming round the collar and pocket flaps?'

Thrilled at the idea, Bessie nodded her head eagerly.

That very night, Mrs Miners looked out the old coat and started unpicking its seams. Bessie could see that it was a lot of work, but she knew that her mother was enjoying making her something new. Even though they had a big family - Bessie was the eighth of twelve children - somehow their parents made each one feel special.

Although Bessie's new coat was ready the following Friday, she decided that she wouldn't wear it until Sunday, so that it would get its very first showing at church. 'We must look like a snake winding its way along the road,' one of her brothers teased, as they walked to the morning service. 'There is such a long string of us!' Bessie laughed. This was her favourite day of the week. The family was all together. There was no school, and the house was full of joy. When Bessie was a grown-up thinking back to her childhood home, she often remembered the joy she had known there.

'Do you really like going to church so

often?' a friend asked Bessie, the following Monday. The girl looked surprised at the question. 'Yes,' she said. 'I love it! Don't you?'

Her friend scowled. 'I don't,' she grumbled. 'Sunday's a horrible day. We're not allowed to do anything interesting and the church services are so boring.'

Bessie was shocked at the idea. 'I've never even been bored on a week-day!' she laughed. 'And Sundays in our home are really special. Usually we all gather round the old pump organ and sing together.' 'Ugh!' her friend said. 'You mean you have another service at home!'

'Will you come to the shop with me,' her friend asked, some time later. Bessie was happy to do that, but what happened in the shop troubled her for months until she could sort it out. Having bought what she went for, her friend was about to leave the shop counter when she noticed a shilling lying on it. Quick as a flash she picked it up and put it in her pocket.

'Look what I've got!' the girl told Bessie, when they were a safe distance away. Bessie's eyes nearly popped out of her head at the sight of the shilling! 'Let's go and buy sweets,' her friend suggested. 'Then we'll find a den and eat them.'

Because Bessie came from such a big family, there was rarely any money for sweets. She went along with her friend and watched as she chose chocolate and candy bars. Then the pair of them headed for their den to eat them. But even as the chocolate melted in her mouth, Bessie's enjoyment of it melted away. Although she hadn't stolen the money, she knew that what she was doing was wrong. It took her a long time to do it, but she saved up a shilling and returned it to the lady who ran the shop.

By the time Bessie was twelve years old she knew a lot about money. She knew that you didn't have to have much to be happy, and that although her parents had no extra money at all, God had always given the whole family all that they needed. From the escapade with the shilling she learned that money you should not have brings no enjoyment at all.

When Bessie was 16 years old she was sitting one day in church when her life changed completely.

'God really spoke to my heart,' she explained to her friend, the following morning. 'I got up and walked to the front of the church because I wanted to ask the Lord Jesus to forgive my sins and to save me.'

Her friend looked puzzled. 'But you're not a sinner!' she said. 'You've never been brave enough to do anything wrong!' Bessie explained that she was a sinner - that she had done, said, and thought many wrong things - and that she needed to be forgiven before she could go to heaven. 'You'll be wanting to be a missionary before long!' her friend teased.

Something in Bessie's heart thrilled at the very thought.

'Good afternoon,' a warm Irish voice said. Bessie looked up from the counter of the little restaurant in which she worked. 'Good afternoon,' she replied. 'What can I get you?'

After serving the young man, the two got into conversation. He was a preacher, and they found themselves talking about their faith. What he said made a great impression on the girl.

'Lord,' Bessie prayed, after her customer had paid his bill and left, 'I'll do anything you want me to do. I'll be anything you want me to be. I'll go anywhere you want me to go.'

And having prayed that prayer, Bessie wondered what God would do with her life. From the rugged coastline of her home village of Porthleven, Bessie could look out to the English Channel. Most often what caught her eye was her father's fishing boat, but from time to time she saw a ship voyaging west.

'I wonder where that's going,' she would

find herself thinking. 'Maybe it's making its way to Africa or India or the South Sea Islands. Perhaps one day God will call me to go abroad as a missionary for him, and the family will watch my ship heading out past the Isles of Scilly to the Atlantic Ocean.'

Bessie smiled at that memory when God did show her what he wanted her to do. And he used another customer at the restaurant to point her in the right direction. He was with a group called the Friends Evangelistic Band, that toured rural villages telling people about Jesus. When she thought about the work they did, she knew in her heart that she should join them.

'But I'd need to leave home,' she worried. 'And my family mean so much to me. I just can't imagine not being with them. Can God really be calling me to do that?'

Bessie thought about it, prayed about it, and eventually talked to her minister, before coming to a final decision.

'I believe that God's calling me to join the Friends Evangelistic Band,' she told her parents. 'But the minister doesn't agree,' she added honestly.

Bessie's father smiled gently. 'He told me so. I'm afraid he doesn't think a young woman should be touring the country in a horse-drawn gypsy caravan, even if she has another young woman with her. Nor does he think you should work for a group that doesn't pay its workers.'

'God will supply all I need,' Bessie said confidently.

Her parents smiled. 'We agree with you,' her mother said. 'He's supplied all we've ever needed. If that's what you feel God wants you to do, then do it with our blessing.'

The horse-drawn caravan became a well-known sight in Cornish villages, and Bessie and her fellow missionaries were welcomed as they travelled round the country lanes. 'Look what I found!' she exclaimed, when they arrived back from visiting a village. 'This was under the caravan step.' Opening the basket, they discovered it was full of good things: six eggs, a newly-baked loaf, a tin of corned beef, some milk, and a little money wrapped in a twist of brown paper. Sitting on the grass beside the basket, the two young women thanked God for giving them just what they needed.

In 1938, a young man appeared on the scene, one who was doing the same kind of work. His name was Kenneth Adams, and just three months later Bessie became his wife. After their wedding they went off on a touring honeymoon, eventually arriving at Campbeltown on the west of Scotland, where

Kenneth had held missionary meetings the previous year. As they sat on the slopes of Beinn Ghuilean overlooking Campbeltown Loch, they talked about their hopes and plans for the future. They didn't know where God would lead them, or exactly the kind of work he wanted them to do, but they felt it right to make an important decision about their future. Within a few days of being married, they committed themselves to doing God's work without receiving any payment... because they believed that God would provide everything they needed. And he did, as they discovered while they toured the villages Bessie had grown to love. Their home was another gypsy caravan, and their equipment was a tent that could seat 150 people, and a big box of Christian books. What they didn't know was that the books held the key to an amazing future together.

The young missionaries were just coming to the conclusion that God could really use a Christian literature team when a letter arrived. It had 'Confidential' written on the envelope.

'I think I know what this is about,' Kenneth said.

Bessie smiled. 'So do I.'

They opened the letter to find they were both correct. The Friends Evangelistic Band had written asking them to establish a literature

Bessie Adams

ministry to service its travelling workers. Kenneth and Bessie gladly agreed to give up their village meetings for a year to start the new work, if they would be allowed to go back to their gypsy life thereafter. But God had other plans.

The literature work grew, and the young couple knew that God wanted them to continue in it. Eventually, when they took over the work and founded Christian Literature Crusade (CLC) in 1941, they could never have guessed what the outcome would be. Two years later, someone wrote an article suggesting that they should aim to have 200 Christian bookshops, and become a kind of 'spiritual Woolworths'! Kenneth and Bessie swallowed hard because they were wise enough to recognise the danger of things growing too quickly.

Within 20 years CLC had grown and spread to many countries of the world, and Kenneth and Bessie had made their home in Fort Washington, near Philadelphia, U.S.A. By then they had two daughters, Margaret and Janet, who became very used to waving their father goodbye as he set off on his travels to visit the ever-expanding shops and workers of CLC.

'Do you mind Kenneth being away so often?' someone asked Bessie one day.

She smiled before answering. 'Of course I miss him a lot,' she said. 'But he was the Lord's before he was mine, so I can hardly complain about him doing the Lord's work.' The friend had another question she wanted to ask. 'Do you not mind that he's able to do missionary work while you're left here at home?'

Bessie looked seriously at the person who had asked the question, then her face broke into a smile. 'My dear,' she said kindly. 'I don't know what my husband has done this morning, but I've already spoken to two people about the Lord.'

Her friend looked shamefaced. 'That was a really stupid question,' she admitted. 'Of all the people I've ever met, you are the one who speaks to most people about Jesus.' When Margaret and Janet were old enough, Bessie began to join Kenneth on his travels. But she never felt any more a missionary when she was abroad than she did when she was at home.

CLC spread throughout the world, with all of its workers relying on God to supply their needs. Bibles and challenging Christian books were not only sold from shops, but also from market stalls and barrows. Kenneth and Bessie visited as many of the workers as they possibly could. Their passports were full of interesting stamps from which you could almost make an alphabet of places. Among other countries God built up the work of CLC in Africa, Brazil, Chile, Dominica, Europe, Finland, Guyana, Hong Kong, Indonesia, Japan, Korea, Liberia, Mozambique, New Zealand, Panama, Romania, Scotland, Thailand, Uruguay, Venezuela and Wales. Perhaps one day CLC will also work in countries beginning with O, Q, X, Y and Z!

'You could have been a wealthy woman with a worldwide chain of shops,' someone commented to Kenneth and his wife, when they were old enough to retire but still working.

'I am,' Bessie replied. 'I may have no money except what we need today, but I have all the love of a worldwide family and the riches of heaven to look forward to one day. You can't be richer than that!'

Bessie died in 1986, and she is now enjoying all of heaven's riches in the presence of Jesus whom she loved and served.

Fact File: *Passports.* Bessie's husband Kenneth travelled all over the world because of his work with CLC. If you want to travel from one country to another, you need a passport. This is a small book with your photo and some information about you. It is important because it gives proof of identity, which means that people can't enter or leave countries illegally. When you enter a foreign country, they will often put a stamp in your passport to show that you have visited that country.

Keynote: Bessie never had much money. Even when she was a little girl, her family was large and they did not have a lot of money. She learned, after her friend stole the shilling, that money itself does not make us happy, especially if the money is not really ours. She never had a job with a settled wage although she worked hard for all of her adult life. Bessie never lacked anything that she needed. God always provided for her and those around her. God will always provide for those who trust in him.

Think: Bessie's friend thought that she might be frustrated because her husband was travelling all over the world doing missionary work while she had to stay at home. Bessie was able to show her that she could talk to people about Jesus in everyday situations too. God can use us wherever we are, even when the situation doesn't seem very fancy or glamorous. Think about ways in which you can try to serve God where you are just now.

Prayer: Lord Jesus, thankyou for providing all that we need to live. Please help me to remember to thank you for my food and all the other practical things that you give me. Thankyou for the gospel and for the hope that it gives us. Help me to believe it with all of my heart and mind. Amen.

Betty Greene

Betty lay on her back on the grass looking up into the air. High above her two birds swooped and circled above the trees. She turned on her side and looked at her twin brother. Bill, who had closed his eyes against the glare of the sun, had fallen asleep. Seven-year-old Betty took a long piece of grass and tickled his ear with it. Bill jerked in his sleep, then settled down again. His sister waited for a minute then tickled him once again. The boy sat up abruptly. Thinking that an insect had crawled into his ear, he asked his sister to check. It was only when she burst out laughing that he realised the tickling had not been an insect at all, but his twin sister up to her usual tricks.

'Serves you right for falling asleep when there are things to see and do,' she told him.

'It's too warm to do anything,' Bill retorted, 'and there's nothing to see.'

'Yes there is,' Betty argued, pointing high in the sky. 'There are two birds up there and

I've been watching them for ages. They must see something on the ground because they keep circling over the same place.'

Bill shaded his eyes with his hand then lay back to watch the birds with his sister.

'I wonder what it's like being a bird,' he said. 'You'd think they would have to flap their wings really hard to keep up in the air, but their wings hardly seem to be moving.'

'I was reading a book about condors,' commented Betty. 'They are huge, but when they fly the air thermals help to support them so they can go for long distances without flapping their wings at all.'

Bill grinned. 'That sounds like fun. Imagine flying high in the air above here. We could spy on Joe and Albert, and then keep them guessing how we knew what they'd been doing.'

Betty wasn't sure that their older brothers would be all that interesting to watch from the air!

That evening Betty stretched out on her bed to read more about condors. She discovered that they lived in South America, and that they were most common in the mountains of the High Andes. The book had some good pictures in it, and her imagination took over when she closed it and tried to get to sleep. That night she dreamed about South America. In her dream she was high in the air looking down on the River Amazon as it snaked through the jungle far below. From her great height she could see tiny clearings in the rain forest where villages nestled, each a long way from its neighbour. She dreamed that she swooped down above the villages and saw the people who lived in them. Betty was just about to perch on a tree to take a closer look, when her mother called to tell her it was morning. Taking a quick glance at her condor book before climbing out of bed, she discovered that her dream was exactly like a picture in the book!

'Do you know anything about the people who live in the Andes?' she asked her father at breakfast. She was glad it was Saturday and that she didn't have to rush off to school.

Mr Greene thought for a moment. 'I'll tell you what I know,' he said. 'From about the 1200s to the 1530s a very advanced civilization called the Incas lived in parts of South America. They built wonderful cities, some of which can still be seen today. Because of the direction their buildings face, it's thought that they were sun worshippers. But, in the 1530s, the Spaniards invaded their lands. That was called the Spanish Conquest. Sadly the invaders brought diseases like measles with them, and many of the Incas who were not killed in the fighting died of diseases the Europeans carried.'

'Do people there still worship the sun?' Bill asked, fascinated by the story he had just heard.

'There may be some who still do,' Mr Greene said, 'for there are many parts of South America where nobody has yet gone to tell the people about the Lord Jesus.'

'But why don't missionaries go there?' puzzled the boy.

Mr Greene sipped his coffee before answering. 'I'll have to give you a short geography lesson if you are to understand the answer to your questions,' he said. 'Much of South America is covered in rain forest, and many thousands of little villages are dotted around the deepest parts of the forest. There are no roads to most of them. Those that are on rivers sometimes have visits from missionaries who reach them by canoe, but getting to the villages in the dense jungle is much harder. No one has yet worked out how to reach them.'

'But how do you know the villages exist if nobody has ever gone to them?' asked Bill.

His father smiled.

'It's amazing what we've discovered

about remote parts of the country since aeroplanes were invented,' he said.

Betty listened carefully to what her father was saying. 'I know another way of reaching these villages,' she thought, as she helped her mother clear the breakfast things. 'You could travel by condor!'

Just a few months later, the Greene family piled into their car and headed to the University of Washington to watch history being made.

'Do you think he'll make it?' Bill asked.

Mr Greene smiled. 'I sure do,' he said. 'In just a few hours, when Charles Lindbergh lands at Sand Point Naval Station, he'll be the first person to fly non-stop across the Atlantic Ocean. 1927 will be remembered for this huge step in the progress of flight.'

'Where did he start from?' Betty wanted to know.

Her twin was able to answer that. 'He's flown from Paris. And if he arrives on time, the flight will have taken 33 or 34 hours. Imagine crossing the Atlantic in that time!'

Betty smiled. 'I can't wait to see his aeroplane. *The Spirit of St Louis* is such a lovely name.'

Soon they joined the thousands of others who had gathered to watch Lindbergh arrive.

'There he is!' yelled Bill. 'Look!'

Everyone followed his finger, and one by one people saw the tiny dot in the distance. All eyes were fixed on the silver monoplane as it circled in the air before landing at Sand Point. Cheers rose from the crowd. But they were nothing to the cheer that greeted Lindbergh when he was driven back to the stadium for the recognition ceremony.

That night Betty didn't dream of condors. Instead, she saw herself climbing into the cockpit of a silver monoplane and flying off into the far blue yonder. Over the years that followed, Betty dreamed about flying even when she was wide awake, which may be why their parents gave Bill and Betty a flight in an aeroplane for their 16th birthday present.

At the beginning of the Second World War, Betty Greene joined the Women Airforce Service Pilots. Flying training could be dangerous in those days, as one of her friends found out. Betty wrote home about it. 'Today I saw a PT-19 taxi up to the line with the instructor in the rear cockpit and no-one in the front - only earphones hanging over the side blowing in the wind. One of my classmates, as she levelled from a spin, had floated out of the cockpit when her safety belt failed! Thankfully she managed to pull the rip cord on her parachute and land safely.' Betty did so well in her basic training that she became a test pilot and engaged in high altitude flying.

'God saved my life,' she told her friend Ann, when she landed one afternoon.

Ann looked concerned.

'We flew up into the stratosphere to conduct tests on oxygen masks and electric flying suits,' explained Betty. 'All the windows and doors were open and a bitterly cold wind whisked through the plane. All sorts of tests were going on with various bits of equipment. Suddenly I noticed that the needle on my oxygen bottle registered zero! I wasn't getting any oxygen at all.'

'That could have been fatal,' Ann said, in a shocked voice.

Betty nodded. 'I signalled to the lieutenant in charge and he came immediately. I held my breath and he helped me crush the ice that had formed in the intake tube, and shake it out. I was desperate for breath by the time I was connected up again.'

That night, as Betty lay in her bed, she thought over what had happened. Her heart just overflowed with love for God who had saved her life as well as saving her soul. 'What,' wondered Betty, 'does my heavenly Father want me to do with my life? Whatever it is, I'll do it with all my heart.' And as she lay in the darkness she remembered what the Lord Jesus had done for her.

When the Women Airforce Service Pilots were disbanded in December 1944, Betty knew what God wanted her to do. She became the first woman pilot to join Christian Airmen's Missionary Fellowship. (CAMF later changed its name to Mission Aviation Fellowship, as that was the name used by the sister organisation in the United Kingdom.) As Betty was increasing her flying hours high in the air, missionary translators worked on the ground in many parts of Central and South America, creating written languages from those that, till then, had only been spoken. CAMF was asked to help transport these people, and as Betty was the only free pilot, she was delegated to make the organisation's first flight into Mexico.

'February 23, 1946,' she wrote in her diary. 'Today I started out for Mexico in a beautiful red four-seater Waco biplane. Both my passengers were as excited as I was. Maximum speed - just over 100 miles per hour. Arrived safety at Phoenix.'

Every day she added details of the flight to her diary. After many stops for refuelling, the biplane reached Mexico City. Betty Greene had made history! But she was not allowed a holiday just because of that; the following day she was in the air again, taking a missionary to the south of Mexico.

Betty Greene

'It's solid jungle down there,' Mr Townsend said.

Betty looked down at the beauty of it. Suddenly the biplane's engine died. Time seemed to freeze, and the silence was deafening. Betty scanned the ground for a possible landing site, but there was none. Then she switched fuel tanks and pressed the starter. The engine fired up immediately. She looked over at her passenger only to find him as calm as he had been before, and still enjoying the view!

A few months later, Betty was asked to fly in Peru, and on December 19th she tackled her toughest assignment so far - a flight over the Andes mountains.

'It was an amazing experience,' she told her friends later. 'From Lima we climbed through a 10,000 feet cloud blanket before reaching clear skies. But that was just the beginning of our climb. At 12,000 feet I put on my oxygen mask and we were still climbing. It was so clear at 16,000 feet I felt I could have touched the trees below us. Suddenly we hit a cloudbank, and visibility was non-existent. I brought the plane down below cloud level and flew along the broad back of the mountain. Then, as I looked down on the forest with its tiny village clearings, I suddenly remembered my childhood dream. I saw what condors see on their flights over the high Andes! I could see tiny villages to which missionaries could be taken with the help of a plane, villages that were virtually inaccessible otherwise.'

Although she didn't know it at the time, Betty Greene had made history once again. She was the first woman pilot to cross the Andes and to fly in the rain forest.

Betty Greene's service with Mission Aviation Fellowship was not limited to Central and South America. In February 1951, she moved to Nigeria where she flew as an MAF pilot on loan to a missionary society. Her next assignment took her to the Sudan. Then, in 1958, she travelled south to work in Irian Jaya (That's the west side of the huge island of New Guinea, which is north and east of Australia. Papua New Guinea is the east side of the island). As well as transporting missionaries and local Christian workers, she was involved in airlifting seriously ill patients to hospital, taking food to remote villages where there was famine or drought, and ferrying medical teams, equipment and supplies to hospitals and clinics in rural areas.

Betty's influence continued long after her flying career ended. George Boggs, a former

Betty Greene

MAF pilot, said, 'Betty Greene had a dream of reaching the remotest places on earth for the Lord through the use of airplanes ... It was she who gave me that first missionary pilot inspiration.' And George was not the only MAF pilot to have taken to the air after being inspired by the story of Betty Greene. Another former MAF pilot, Chuck Bennett, commented, 'Betty Greene was the first to fly across the Andes, and the first missionary pilot to fly in Mexico, Peru and Nigeria. Without a doubt she was the most amazing women I've ever known.'

Today Mission Aviation Fellowship has over 150 aircraft flying in 30 of the poorest countries. Every three minutes an MAF plane takes off or lands somewhere in the world, and each in its own way brings help and hope to the people it serves.

Factfile: *The Andes.* Betty Greene was the first woman to fly across the Andes, the longest mountain range in the world. It stretches all the way from near the Caribbean Sea to Cape Horn, at the very south of South America. For much of their length they are over 12, 000 feet high– nearly three times as high as Ben Nevis, the highest mountain in Britain. The height of the Andes means that some of the weather conditions there are very extreme. Towns such as Arica in Chile may only have rain once every hundred years!

Keynote: Betty had seen Charles Lindbergh make history when he crossed the Atlantic in The Spirit of *St Louis* but she made history herself a few times in the course of her work with MAF. She didn't set out to break records or make history, it just happened as she tried to serve God. We don't need to try to make ourselves important. What really matters is serving

Betty Greene

God, but we might find that we end up doing some important things as we try to serve him.

 Think: Betty nearly died when her oxygen pipe became blocked with ice during the test flight. She realised that she had only survived because God had saved her life, and that she should live her whole life for him. Betty was keen to do whatever God wanted her to do with all her heart. It is important to be enthusiastic about doing what God asks us to do. It would be very ungrateful to grudge obeying someone who has done so much for us. Think about things that you can thank God for.

 Prayer: Lord Jesus, thankyou for all that you have done for me. Please help me to do all that I can to serve you. Show me all of the ways that you have blessed me so that I can be thankful for them. Please help those who are working with MAF planes today. Amen.

Elisabeth Elliot

As the sun poured through the window Elisabeth could see tiny specs of dust floating in the air. She blew gently, and those close to her danced before settling down to float once again. Raising her hand to catch one, she noticed that the movement sent them spinning upwards as though they were trying to get away from her.

'Look Mum,' she said, as the room door opened, 'aren't they beautiful?'

Mrs Howard smiled. 'They are indeed,' she agreed. 'But if I came over to see them from where you are, I'd knock them in all directions and you would lose their beauty.'

'Why do lovely things have to change and go away?' the six-year-old asked. 'Why can't they always be there for us?'

Sitting down on a seat near the window, Mrs Howard smiled kindly at her daughter. 'I think you know the reason for that,' she suggested.

Puzzled, Elisabeth turned in her direction. Then she puzzled even more.

'I suppose everything was always beautiful when Adam and Eve were in the Garden of Eden,' she said.

Her mother nodded. 'And in a way that we don't understand every single thing was changed when they disobeyed God. Everything became less beautiful.'

'But there are still nice things in the world,' the child insisted.

Mrs Howard agreed. 'There certainly are, and each one of them is a gift from God for us to treasure.'

When Elisabeth went to bed that night her heart was heavy. The next day she was going to a new school, and that felt very scary. As she lay in bed she remembered back to an awful day not long after she went to Miss Dietz's kindergarten, which was just round the corner from her home.

'I loved playing with the little china cat in the toy box there,' she remembered. 'I played all kinds of pretend games with it. Often I used the building bricks to make a home for it. Then one day another girl got the white china cat first. I tried to snatch it from her, but she ran away with the cat.'

Even in the dark Elisabeth blushed at the memory of what happened next.

'I chased after her, shouting that the china cat was mine. Miss Dietz soon put a stop to both our nonsense, and told me very firmly that the cat was not mine at all. It was for all of the children in the kindergarten to play with.'

There was a lump in her throat that made Elisabeth feel she might cry.

'It was horrible,' she remembered. 'Although I'd had rows from Dad and Mum for being naughty, it was much worse to get a row from someone else ... and in front of all my friends.'

Before the girl went to sleep that night, she made up her mind that she would try to be very, very good at her new school. Everything might be less beautiful than it was in the Garden of Eden, but she was determined to make her tiny part of the world beautiful.

The following morning Elisabeth wakened with a funny feeling in her tummy, and a hundred thoughts in her mind.

'I won't know where to go in Henry School. I'll get lost there. I'll not understand the arithmetic. I don't know anybody. Nobody will want to be my friend.'

Mrs Howard prayed with her anxious little daughter before she went off to school that day. And God answered her prayers in the gift of Miss Scott.

'My teacher's lovely!' Elisabeth told her parents, when she arrived home. 'She has a soft voice and snow-white hair. And she can make rainbows!'

'How does she do that?' asked her father.

Elisabeth smiled at the memory.

'When the sun shone through the high sashed windows, Miss Scott turned a crystal prism that hung on one of the shade pulls and suddenly the room was filled with lots of rainbows. She even let us try to catch them!'

Her parents looked at each other and smiled.

'And do you know what?' Elisabeth added excitedly. 'Miss Scott says that sometimes, when we've been very very good, she might make more rainbows for us to catch!'

Henry School was a dismal building, and the road between home and school was no better. But Elisabeth knew that even there God had given her something beautiful. And although she, like all the others in her class, sometimes found school work difficult, Miss Scott was there to help. She didn't have to cope all on her own. As she grew older and trusted in the Lord Jesus for herself, she discovered again and again that although life was sometimes difficult he was always there to help her.

'Have you always lived in Philadelphia?' a friend asked one day, when they were thirteen years old.

'No,' Elisabeth said. 'I was born in Brussels.'

'Where's that?' the other girl queried, not being too good at geography.

'Brussels is in Belgium,' Elisabeth explained.

'Isn't that dangerously near Germany?' enquired her friend. 'My dad says that Hitler will soon invade all the countries round about Germany because he wants to conquer the whole of Europe.'

Thinking back to her parents' concern for their Belgian friends, Elisabeth agreed that Philadelphia was a safer place than Brussels in 1939.

'Why were your parents in Belgium when you were born?' the other girl asked.

'They were missionaries there,' Elisabeth explained.

'That must be hard work,' her friend commented. 'Imagine having to speak in a different language all the time.'

Elisabeth was fascinated by different languages, and the ones that especially interested her were those that were still unwritten.

'How do people make a written language from one that's only spoken?' she asked her father.

Mr Howard tried his best to answer his daughter's question.

'They have to live with the people and listen hard to everything that's said. Spending time with mothers and children is often a great help to them. Tiny bit by tiny bit they pick up words and phrases, trying out each one over and over to make sure they really do understand its meaning. People are often pleased that a stranger from another country is interested in their language, and then they do their best to help.'

'How do they decide how the words should be written?' queried the girl.

'I don't think there's a problem with sounds that are also in our language, but they have to use symbols other than the English alphabet for sounds we don't have.'

'Give me an example,' said Elisabeth, who was really interested in what she was hearing.

Mr Howard scratched his head as he thought of an example. Then he smiled.

'Some languages have clicks in them,' he told his daughter, 'so they have to use other symbols to represent those.'

The writing down of unwritten languages became Elisabeth's chief interest, and when grown-ups asked her what she wanted to do with her life, she always told them she wanted to do that more than anything else. When she went to Wheaton to study, she majored in

Greek because she knew that would help her. Another student was studying Greek for the same reason. His name was Jim Elliot. When she was 22, in 1948, Elisabeth spent the summer at an Institute of Linguistics before moving to Canada to attend missionary training college. In 1952, Jim Elliot and Elisabeth Howard left separately for Ecuador as mission workers. Elisabeth went to the western jungle to work among the Colorado Indians, and Jim went to the eastern jungle and the Quichua people. Although the young couple were deeply attracted to each other, they wanted to know for sure that God's will was for them to marry. Doing what God wanted them to do was more important to them than their love for each other.

'Some of the trees are wonders for size and majesty,' Jim wrote, in one of his many letters to Elisabeth. 'One, that we can see on the other side of the airstrip from the house, has roots which run away from the trunk like walls, bracing the height like structural triangles. I have seen one of these uchu putus with holes five feet across in the roots, where the Indians have hacked out a piece of wood for their huge trays, which they use for mashing chonta fruit, or as a butcher's block.'
The airstrip Jim mentioned was his lifeline, because the area in which he and a

small group of other missionaries worked was very remote indeed.

'I was sitting as usual at a little table in a thatched-roofed house in the western jungle, working over my Colorado language notes,' Elisabeth wrote later, 'when suddenly the sound of horse's hoofs broke through the clicking, singing, rattling, and buzzing of the night noises. I took the lantern outside, and was greeted by a friend from a village about eight miles away. He handed me a telegram. Jim was waiting for me in Quito!'

Jim's next letter home explained the reason for his visit.

'I gave Betty an engagement ring last night,' he told his parents.

They were married in 1953, and God gave them a daughter, Valerie, two years later.

'Do you think it would be possible to reach the Auca Indians?' Jim asked his young wife. 'They have a terrible reputation for violence, but they need to hear about the Lord Jesus just as much as anyone else. We can't just shy away from them because of their reputation ... or,' he added, 'because of our fears.'

Elisabeth prayed about the Auca people, and waited to see what would happen. Jim's desire to reach them grew as time passed, until he was absolutely sure that was what God wanted done.

Elisabeth Elliot

'Nate Saint, from Mission Aviation Fellowship, is prepared to help us,' Jim told his wife. 'But we need to make our plans most carefully.'

Knowing the dangers involved, but remembering what she had learned as a child - that Jesus is right with his people when things are difficult – Elisabeth backed up all the plans with her prayers. Four other missionaries' wives did the same.

Nate flew the MAF light aircraft low over the Auca settlement many, many times to accustom the people to their visitors. Then gifts were lowered in a bucket to show that they were friendly. The message seemed to get through, because eventually some little gifts were put in the bucket for the missionaries. How thrilled they were when that happened! The day that Jim, Nate and their fellow missionaries had looked forward to for so long came eventually in January 1956. They had agreed on a riverside landing site, and they went off to meet the Auca Indians face to face.

What happened when the missionaries and the Auca people came in contact is hard to write about. Elisabeth described it later.

'About 11 o'clock on Friday 6th January, Nate and Pete sat in the small cooking shelter they had built on the sand. Ed was at the upper end of the beach, Rog in the centre, Jim at the lower end. They were calling out Auca words in case anyone was within hearing range. At 11.15 their hearts jumped when a man's voice boomed out from across the river. Immediately three Aucas stepped into the open. They were a young man, and two women. Amazed, the missionaries managed to shout, in Auca, "Puinani!", which means "welcome". Before long the three had joined the missionaries and many "punanis" and smiles were exchanged. Things looked hopeful.'

With a final radio message back to their wives, the five men set out on the greatest adventure of their lives. They did meet some of the Auca people. But while Jim and his friends took with them the good news that Jesus saves, the Indians brought wooden spears with which they killed God's messengers. Jim Elliot, Nate Saint, Ed McCully, Rog Youderian and Pete Fleming one minute saw the faces of their killers, and the next their lovely Lord Jesus. Having been martyred for him here on earth they were immediately taken home to heaven.

'To the world at large this was a sad waste of five young lives,' Elisabeth wrote later. 'But God has his plan and purpose in all things.'

After spending a short time at home in America, Elisabeth went back to Equador to continue working on the Quetchua language.

Elisabeth Elliot

With little Valerie she made her home there. Later, with Rachel Saint (Nate's widow) they moved back to live and work with the Auca people for a time. Elisabeth rediscovered what she had learned as a child, that there is beauty even in deepest darkness. They grew to love the people, and had the thrill of seeing many trust in the Lord Jesus, even some of those who had been involved in their husbands' murders.

In 2000, the Auca (now called the Waorani) people watched MAF light aircraft carry loads of building materials into their region of Ecuador. On the ground, men and boys were already beginning to build what was to become a Bible college. There God's good news would be taught to the Waorani people, so that they can tell others that whatever horrible things their past lives hold, Jesus is able to forgive them and save them from their sins. Out of the awful experience through which Elisabeth Elliot and the other four young widows came, something very wonderful was born. From the horrible darkness of terrible sin God can make beautiful things happen.

Fact File: *Bible translators.* One of the main reasons that Elisabeth and her friends worked on writing down the languages of the peoples of South America was to enable them to have the Bible in their own languages. Many Christians have spent a lot of time translating the Bible into various languages. There are still some languages that do not have a Bible translation, but organizations like Wycliffe Bible Translators are working hard to make sure that there will be a translation for every language by 2025.

Keynote: When Elisabeth was little she wondered why beautiful things are so fragile. She later saw that, even in the darkest places that sin can create, God is able to make something beautiful. She found that because Jesus was always there to help her she was never alone. His love and grace can make anyone beautiful. The place where Jim was murdered must have seemed very dark and dangerous to her, but she still had the love and faith to go there and to teach the people about Jesus.

 Think: Elisabeth loved Jim very much. It must have been hard as well as scary for her to go back to the place where he and his friends had been killed. In doing so she was a real example of someone who forgave others for the bad things they had done to her. Jesus tells us to do that. Forgiving people isn't always easy, but that doesn't mean that we shouldn't do it. Try to think of someone whom you can forgive today.

 Pray: Lord Jesus, thankyou for dying so that people can be forgiven for their sins. Help me to remember how great your love and forgiveness is. Please teach me to forgive those who do bad things to me, just as you would want me to. Amen.

Quiz

How much can you remember about these ten girls who made history? Try answering these questions to find out.

Mary Jane Kinnaird

1. What was the special name for the overcrowded building that Mary Jane's uncle visited?

2. Which war did Mary Jane help to train nurses for?

3. What was the name of the organisation that she was involved in setting up to   provide a home for young women coming to London for training and employment?

Emma Dryer

4. Why did Emma want to go walking late at night?

5. What happened to Emma just before she decided to go to Chicago to work for God?

6. What is the name of the Bible college that grew out of Emma's efforts with D.L. Moody to train young people for mission?

Florence Nightingale

7. Which queen did Florence and her sister go to see?

8. What jobs did Florence give to the nurses who went with her to the Crimea when they arrived?

9. What did Florence do after the war to improve army medical services?

Lottie Moon

10. Where was Lottie's uncle going to be a missionary?

11. What kind of subject was Lottie very good at?

12. What happened when the man tried to kill Lottie with a sword?

Ida Scudder

13. Why couldn't Ida's father attend to the Brahmin's wife?

14. What did the Indians call Ida?

15. How many of Ida's first class of students passed the medical exam?

Jeannette Li

16. How old was Mooi Nga when she got married?

17. What was the name of the travelling salesman who became a Christian?

18 Which country occupied China during the Second World War?

Henrietta Mears

19. What illness did Henrietta have when she was a child?

20. What did the girls in Margaret's Sunday school class call themselves?

21. How much did they pay for the campsite that was supposed to be worth $350,000?

Bessie Adams

22. What did Bessie and Kenneth travel in when they were touring the villages?

23. Which Scottish town did they visit at the end of their honeymoon?

24. What does CLC stand for?

Betty Greene

25. What kind of birds did Betty dream about when she was young?

26. What did Bill and Betty get for their 16th birthday present?

27. Which organization did Bessie join after the Second World War?

Elisabeth Elliot

28. What kind of sounds do some languages in South America and Africa have that English doesn't?

29. What language did Elisabeth study to help her with writing down unwritten languages?

30. What were the Indians called who murdered Jim and his friends?

Answers

1. A rookery.

2. The Crimean War.

3. The Young Women's Christian Association.

4. So that she could look at the stars.

5. She was very ill with typhoid fever.

6. The Moody Bible Institute.

7. Queen Victoria

8. Buying vegetables, setting up stoves and cooking food, making bandages and washing the whole hospital.

9. She pushed for the creation of the Army Medical School, which opened in 1860.

10. Jerusalem

11. Languages

12. God stopped him and made him drop his sword.

13. The Brahmin's religion said that female patients could only be attended by female doctors.

Quiz

14. Doctor Amma.

15. All of them.

16. 15

17. Mr Wang.

18. Japan.

19. Muscular Rheumatism.

20. The Snobs.

21. $30,000

22. A gypsy caravan.

23. Campbeltown

24. Christian Literature Crusade.

25. Condors

26. A flight in an aeroplane.

27. Christian Airmen's Missionary Fellowship.

28. Clicks

29. Greek

30. Auca indians.

This is what one man said about

Henrietta Mears

"I doubt if any other woman outside my wife and mother has had such a marked influence on my life. She is certainly one of the greatest Christians I have ever known!" *Billy Graham*

LIGHT KEEPERS

Start collecting this series now!

Ten Boys who Made History

Samuel Rutherford

John Owen

Jonathan Edwards

George Whitefield

Robert Murray McCheyne

Dwight L. Moody

Billy Sunday

Charles H. Spurgeon

Aiden W. Tozer

Martyn Lloyd-Jones

LIGHT KEEPERS

Start collecting this series now!

Ten Boys who Changed the World

David Livingstone, Billy Graham,

Brother Andrew, John Newton,

William Carey, George Müller,

Nicky Cruz, Eric Liddell,

Luis Palau, Adoniram Judson.

Ten Boys who Made a Difference

Augustine of Hippo, Jan Hus,

Martin Luther, Ulrich Zwingli,

William Tyndale, Hugh Latimer,

John Calvin, John Knox,

Lord Shaftesbury, Thomas Chalmers.

LIGHT KEEPERS

Start collecting this series now!

Ten Girls who Changed the World

Corrie Ten Boom, Mary Slessor,

Joni Eareckson Tada, Isobel Kuhn,

Amy Carmichael, Elizabeth Fry,

Evelyn Brand, Gladys Alyward,

Catherine Booth, Jackie Pullinger.

Ten Girls who Made a Difference

Monica of Thagaste, Katherine Luther,

Susanna Wesley, Ann Judson,

Maria Taylor, Susannah Spurgeon,

Bethan Lloyd-Jones, Edith Schaeffer,

Sabina Wurmbrand, Ruth Bell Graham.

Trailblazers

DANGER ON THE HILL

TORCHBEARERS

CATHERINE MACKENZIE

"Run, run for your lives," a young boy screamed. "Run, everybody, run. The soldiers are here."

That day on the hill is the beginning of a new and terrifying life for the three Wilson children. Margaret, Agnes and Thomas are not afraid to stand up for what they believe in, but it means that they are forced to leave their home and their parents for a life of hiding on the hills.

If you were a covenanter in the 1600s you were the enemy of the King and the authorities. But all you really wanted to do was worship God in the way he told you to in the Bible. Margaret wants to give Jesus Christ the most important place in her life, and this conviction might cost her life.

There is danger on the hill for MARGARET; There is danger everywhere - if you are a covenanter.

The Torchbearers series are true life stories form history where Christians have suffered and died for their faith in Christ.

ISBN 1 85792 7842

CHRISTIAN FOCUS

Staying faithful - Reaching out!

Christian Focus Publications publishes books for adults and children under its three main imprints: Christian Focus, Mentor and Christian Heritage. Our books reflect that God's word is reliable and Jesus is the way to know him, and live forever with him.

Our children's publication list includes a Sunday school curriculum that covers pre-school to early teens; puzzle and activity books. We also publish personal and family devotional titles, biographies and inspirational stories that children will love.

If you are looking for quality Bible teaching for children then we have an excellent range of Bible story and age specific theological books.

From pre-school to teenage fiction, we have it covered!

Find us at our web page:
www.christianfocus.com